A SIMPLIFIED GRAMMAR
OF THE
GUJARATI LANGUAGE

TOGETHER WITH A SHORT READING BOOK AND VOCABULARY

A SIMPLIFIED GRAMMAR OF THE GUJARATI LANGUAGE

TOGETHER WITH A SHORT READING BOOK AND VOCABULARY

William St. Clair Tisdall

ISBN : 978-93-5324-519-1 (HB)

First Published, 1892

Published, 2020

Published by

Facsimile Publisher
12 Pragati Market
Ashok Vihar, Ph-2
Delhi-110052
E-mail: books@facsimilepublisher.com

Printed at: G. Print Process, Delhi.

A Simplified Grammar of the Gujarati Language

Together with A Short Reading Book and Vocabulary

Author: William St. Clair Tisdall

TO

THE MEMBERS

OF THE

IRISH PRESBYTERIAN MISSION, GUJARĀT,

WHO HAVE DONE SO MUCH FOR

GUJARĀTĪ LITERATURE,

THIS LITTLE VOLUME IS, WITHOUT THEIR KNOWLEDGE,

DEDICATED.

PREFACE.

The Series of Simplified Grammars to which the present volume belongs is too well known to make it necessary for me to say much now in the way of preface. I must, however, record my obligations to two vernacular Grammars,—the ગૂજરાતી ભાષાનું વ્યાકરણ of the Rev. J. van S. Taylor, B.A., and another small book of the same title by Sir T. C. Hope, late Educational Inspector, Northern Division. When I had already made good progress in writing the present work, I met with "A Handbook of Gujarātī Grammar," by P. M. Bhatt, from which I was able to borrow a few useful hints. But a perusal of the Grammar now offered to the public will show that I have not followed any of these works in a servile spirit.

There seems at present to be a great dearth of English works on the Gujarātī language. When I began to study that language in Bombay a few years ago, I found it impossible to procure a single copy of any of the earlier Grammars. Nor should I have derived much assistance from them if I had, owing to the great improvements which have of recent years taken place in Gujarātī spelling. I trust that students of Gujarātī will find that this little book supplies a real need. The transliterational system employed in the Grammar is an exact one, so that no confusion can arise from the use of English letters to represent Gujarātī words.

I hope but few errors of the press will be found to have escaped detection, and that the system of transliteration that I have adopted will prevent those few from causing the student any real inconvenience.

W. St. C. T.

London, *Jan.*, 1892.

INDEX.

PART I.

GUJARĀTĪ ACCIDENT, &c.

SPECIMENS OF GOOD GUJARĀTĪ WRITING.

(*From* "DASTAK SHIKSHAK.")

બીજાનું હિત ઇચ્છવું એવી વૃત્તિ સદ્ગુણી મનુષ્યના હૃદયમાં થાયછે.

સૂર્યની આસપાસ પૃથ્વી અમુક નિયમે ફરેછે માટે દિવસ લાંબા ટુંકા થાયછે.

વિદ્વાન્ પુરૂષ વિદ્યાના બળથી અભણ માનવી ઉપર સરસાઈ ભોગવેછે.

જાહેર હિંમતનો સ્તુતિપાત્ર ગુણ ઘણા થોડા માણસોમાં જોવામાં આવેછે.

જેમ પડી રહેલું લોઢું કીટથી ખવાયછે તેમ શરીર આળસથી ખવાયછે.

ખાનપાનને ખાતર જીદગી નથી પણ જીંદગીને ખાતર ખાનપાન છે.

THE ELEMENTS OF THE GRAMMAR

OF THE

GUJARĀTĪ LANGUAGE.

THE Gujarātī language belongs, like the Marāṭhī, Hindī, Panjābī, Oriya, and many other Indian dialects, to the Āryan family, being a daughter of the Sanskṛit. Its closest affinities are with the Western Panjābī on the one side, and the Braj Bhāshā, an old form of Hindī, on the other. Besides various local dialects of Gujarātī, there are three main varieties of the written and spoken language. First, Hindī Gujarātī, which is that adopted—and rightly so—by the Government as the standard, and taught in the schools. Second, Pārsī Gujarātī, the language as spoken and written by the Pārsīs. This differs from ordinary Gujarātī in that it admits pure Persian words in considerable numbers, especially in connexion with religious matters, besides a host of Arabic and other words taken from the Urdū language, and that its grammar is in a very unfixed and irregular condition. Thirdly, Muḥammadan Gujarātī, which, like Pārsī Gujarātī, employs a great number of words borrowed from the Hindūstānī (and through it from Persian and Arabic). But, though the vocabulary of the language varies considerably according as the speaker is a Hindū, a Pārsī, or a Muslim, yet its grammar—when spoken correctly—is practically one and the same. We have taken Hindī Gujarātī as our standard in this Grammar, for, if that is learnt, the few variations of form used in the other dialects will present no difficulty, especially as they are to a great degree mere matters of spelling.

GUJARĀTĪ PARADIGMS.

I. Nouns:—

(a) *Masculine.*

(1) Ending in -*o*

	Sing.	*Plur.*
Abs.	——*o*	——*ā*(*o*)
Obl.	——*ā*	——*ā*(*o*)

(2) Otherwise:—

	Sing.	*Plur.*
Abs.	——	——(*o*)
Obl.	——	——(*o*)

(b) *Feminine.*

	Sing.	*Plur.*
Abs.	——	——*o*
Obl.	——	——*o*

(c) *Neuter.*

(1) Ending in -*uñ*

	Sing.	*Plur.*
Abs.	——*uñ*	——*āñ*(*o*)
Obl.	——*ā*	——*āñ*(*o*)

(2) Otherwise:—

	Sing.	*Plur.*
Abs.	——	——(*o*)
Obl.	——	——(*o*)

II. Verbs:—

(a) *Regular.*

Active Stem, ——
Pass. Stem, ˘——*ā*
Causative Stem, ˘—— { *āḍ* / *āva* }

Infinitive, -*vuñ*.
Gerundive, -*vo, vī, vuñ*.
Present Part., -*to, tī, tuñ; tā, tī, tāñ*.
Past Part., -*yo, ī, yuñ; yā, ī, āñ*.
Connect. Part., -*īne*.
Agential { declin., -*nār-o*, -*ī*, -*uñ*. / indecl., -*nār*. }
Pluperf. Part., -*el*: *el-o*, -*ī*, -*uñ*.
Imperative, -, -*o*.
Aorist, —— + personal endings.
Present Indic. = Aorist + pres. of √*chha*.
Future, —— + -*īś*, -*śe*, -*śe*: -*īśuñ*, -*śo*, -*śe*.
Future Prec., 3rd Sing. and 2nd Pl., -*jo*.
—— Imperat., 2nd Sing. and 2nd Pl., -*je*, -*jo*.

PERSONAL ENDINGS.

	Aorist. 1	2	3	Optative. 3
Sing.,	-uñ	-e	-e	-o
Plur.,	-īe	-o	-e	-o

(b) *Auxiliaries—Irregular.*

(1) √*chha*, to be
Indecl. Pres. Part., *chhatāñ*
Present: *chh-uñ, -e, -e; -īe, -o, -e.*
} Negative, *nathī.*

(2) *Hovuñ*, to be.

Past, *hat-o, -i, -uñ*, &c.

Aorist, *ho-uñ, -y, -y; -īe, -o, -y.*

Fut., *haīś, hoīś*, &c.

Prec. Fut., *hojo.*

(3) *Javuñ*, to go, and *Thavuñ*, to become.

Aorist: *jāuñ, jāy, jāy; jaīe, jāo, jāy.*
thăuñ, thāy, thāy; thaīe, thāo, thāy.

Future: *jaīś*, &c.
thaīś, &c.

III. PRONOUNS:—

(a) *Relative:*—

	Sing.	*Plur.*
Abs.	*je*	*jeo*
Obl.	*je*	*jeo*
Agent.	*jeṇe*	*jeoe*

(b) *Interrog.:*—

	Sing. & Plur.
Abs.	*koṇ*
Obl.	{ *ko-*, *ke-*, *koṇa*

(c) *Reflexive:*—

	Sing. & Plur.
Abs.	*pote*
Obl.	*potā*

(d) *Personal:*—

	Sing.	*Plur.*
1st,	*huñ, mane, meñ, māre, māro*	*ame, amne, ame, amāro*
2nd,	*tuñ, tane, teñ, tāre, tāro*	*tame, tamne, tame, tamāro*
3rd,	*te, tene, teṇe, teno.*	*teo, teone (temne), teono*, &c.

1st Pers. Inclus. plur. pronoun:
Āpaṇe, āpaṇne, āpaṇe, āpaṇo, āpaṇāthī, &c.

IV. SIMPLE POSTPOSITIONS:—

-ne = to, acc.	*-no, -nī, -nuñ* = of.
-e = agent, at.	*-māñ* = in.
-thī = from, with.	*-par* = upon.

CHAPTER I.

The Alphabet.

The Gujarātī Alphabet is derived from the Sanskrit, to which it still bears a considerable resemblance. The difference consists mainly in the omission in Gujarātī of the *head line* used in joining together most of the Devanāgarī characters. Like the Sanskrit, Gujarātī is written *from left to right.*

Letters (*varṇ*) are divided into Vowels (*svar*) and Consonants (*vyanjan, often pronounced venjan*).

§. 1. When *initial,* that is, when they begin a *syllable,* the vowels are as follows :—

અ	= a	pronounced as	*u* in *but.**
આ	= ā	,,	*a* in *army.*
ઇ	= i	,,	*i* in *hit,* but often lengthened in sound.
ઈ	= ī	,,	*ee* in *heel.*
ઉ	= u	,,	*oo* in *hood.*
ઊ	= ū	,,	*oo* in *fool.*
એ	= e	,,	*ê* in *tête,* sometimes almost as *e* in *led.*
ઐ	= ai	,,	*ai* in *aisle.*
ઓ	= o	,,	*o* in *ocean:* always *long.*
ઔ	= au	,,	*ow* in *howl.*

* As this vowel *a* occurs far more frequently in Gujarātī than any other vowel, it is most important that the student should pronounce it correctly, otherwise his conversation will be quite unintelligible.

Or, briefly, the vowels as used by us in transliterating are to be pronounced as in Italian, except that *a* (અ) is to be carefully given the indistinct or *dull* sound indicated above.

When these vowel sounds are *not initial*, they are represented in accordance with the subjoined table. It is to be observed that the first vowel (અ) is supposed to be *inherent* in every consonant, *except*:—(1) when that consonant is followed by some other vowel: (2) when *virāma* (◌્) is written or understood under it: (3) when that consonant is the first portion of a compound letter. Therefore, when this sound *a* (અ) is *not initial*, it possesses no written sign.

NON-INITIAL VOWELS.

Guj.	*Equiv.*			*Name of the character.*
ા	= *ā*,	as બા	= *bā*	... kāno.
િ	= *i*,	„ બિ	= *bi*	... hrasva-ajju.
ી	= *ī*,	„ બી	= *bī*	... dīrgha-ajju.
ુ	= *u*,	„ બુ	= *bu*	... hrasva-varaḍuñ.
ૂ	= *ū*,	„ બૂ	= *bū*	... dīrgha-varaḍuñ.
ે	= *e*,	„ બે	= *be*	... ek mātra.
ૈ	= *ai*,	„ બૈ	= *bai*	... be mātra.
ો	= *o*,	„ બો	= *bo*	... kāno mātra.
ૌ	= *au*,	„ બૌ	= *bau*	... kano be mātra.
ૃ	= *ri*,	„ બૃ	= *bri*	(sounded as *brü*: this *ri* is considered a *vowel*.)

It will be noticed that the sign for short *i* (િ) is always written *before* the consonant which begins the syllable in which it (when not initial) occurs. (The *reverse* of this takes place in the English termination *-ble*, and seems equally strange to a foreigner.)

§ 2. *Simple Consonants.*

CLASS.	CHARACTER.	EQUIV.
GUTTURALS. (kaṇṭhasthānī).	ક	ka
	ખ	kha
	ગ	ga
	ઘ	gha
	ઙ †	ṅ
PALATALS. (tāḷusthānī).	ચ	ch
	છ or છ	chh
	જ	j
	ઝ *	jh
	ઞ †	ñ
CEREBRALS. (murddhāsthānī).	ટ	ṭ
	ઠ	ṭh
	ડ	ḍ
	ઢ	ḍh
	ણ	ṇ
DENTALS. (dantasthānī).	ત	t
	થ	th
	દ	d
	ધ	dh
	ન	n

CLASS.	CHARACTER.	EQUIV.
LABIALS. (oshṭasthānī).	પ	p
	ફ or ફ	f (Some pronounce it as *ph.*)
	બ	b
	ભ	bh
	મ	m
LIQUIDS. (antahstha).	ય	y
	ર	r
	લ	l
	વ	v
ASPIRATES. (ushmā).	શ	ś
	ષ	sh
	સ	s
	હ	h
CEREBRAL LIQUID.	ળ	ḷ

* ઝ઼ is used to transliterate the Persian ژ (*z*) : note the inserted dot.

† The characters marked thus (†) are rarely used in Gujarātī

Some of the characters above given require *two* consonants to represent them in transliteration, and yet they all represent simple and uncompounded sounds. The following require some explanation of their pronunciation:—

ખ *kh*, as in in*k-h*orn, but as if the *k* were part of the *second* syllable.

ગ *g*, is *always hard*, as in *go*.

ઘ *gh*, is a slightly more guttural sound than simple *g*.

The *Cerebrals* are produced by turning the point of the tongue upwards to touch the top of the palate. The letters ઠ (ṭh) and ઢ (ḍh) are somewhat more emphatically pronounced than the simple ટ (ṭ) and ડ (ḍ). The dental *t* and *d* (ત and દ) are softer than the English equivalents, being formed by applying the point of the tongue to the point of the upper teeth. Be careful *not* to give થ (th) and ધ (dh) the sound of English *th* in *thought* and that of *th* in *thou* respectively. *Bh* (ભ) is a more emphatic sound than simple *b* (બ). ફ or ફ઼ is *f*, and not (as the corresponding letter in Sanskrit) *ph*. *Ś* (શ) and (ષ) *sh* have in Gujarātī the same sound, but are vulgarly confounded with simple *s* (સ). *N* before the *aspirates* has always a

—never but in the case of some not properly naturalised Sansk*ri*t words. Those acquainted with Sansk*ri*t will observe that the order and arrangement of the letters in Gujarātī closely follow those of the mother-tongue. Gujarātī adds but one character, cerebral *ḷ* (ળ), to represent a sound not used in classical Sansk*ri*t, though its equivalent ळ is found in the Rig Veda.

nasal sound (as in the French *mon*). *H*, when it comes between two vowels, has a very slight sound, and is often omitted both in speaking and writing. When it is the *first* letter in a compound consonant also, it is hardly audible. *V* (વ) has a sound midway between the English *v* and *w*, but is neither.

Instcad of રૂ and જી respectively, the signs રૂ (*rū*) and જી (*jī*) are used. So also *jā* is written જા, and જુ is *jū*: and રુ is *ru*.

Nasal *n* is written with a dot above the line, as in છોકરૂં (*chhokruñ*). In this Grammar we represent it by *ñ*. The dot is called *anusvār*.

When *n* immediately precedes *b* or *p* it is pronounced as *m*.

The sign : is called *visarga*, and is a final *h*.

The sign ० is used to denote contraction; as ઈ० સ० = i. s. *īsavī san*, = "Christian Year."

R, when the first member of a compound, is written over the following consonant in the form ʿ, as in અર્થે = *arthe*. When it is the second member of a compound, it assumes the form of a simple stroke, as બ્ર = *bra*.

Students acquainted with Arabic or Persian must be careful *not* to give ઘ (*gh*) and ખ (*kh*) the sounds of غ and خ respectively.

§ 3. *Compound Letters.*

These are formed by compounding into one, two or more simple characters. The necessity for their use is because of the rule given above, that અ (ă) is inherent in the sound of every consonant. The compounds are generally easily recognised and read. The most important are given below. The two most difficult are ક્ષ = *ksha*, and જ્ઞ *jna* (pronounced *gnya*).

COMPOUND.	EQUIV.	COMPOUND.	EQUIV.	COMPOUND.	EQUIV.
ક્ત =	*kta*	પ્વ =	*pva*	હ્મ =	*hma*
ક્ન =	*kna*	સ્ત =	*sta*	ઘ્ન =	*ghna*
ક્મ =	*kma*	સ્ત્ર =	*stra*	ઘ્મ =	*ghma*
ક્ય =	*kya*	સ્ર =	*sra*	ટ્ટ =	*ṭṭa*
ક્ર =	*kra*	સ્મ =	*sma*	ઠ્ઠ =	*ṭhṭha*
ગ્વ =	*gva*	સ્ય =	*sya*	દ્દ =	*dda*
ત્ત =	*tta*	સ્વ =	*sva*	ન્સ્ત =	*nsta*
ત્ન =	*tna*	હ્ર =	*hra*	કૃ =	*krĭ*
ત્મ =	*tma*	દ્વ =	*dva*	વ્ય =	*vya*
ત્ય =	*tya*	દ્ય =	*dya*	ષ્ટ =	*shṭa*
ત્ર =	*tra*	દ્ર, દ્ર =	*dra*	હ્ય =	*hya*
ત્વ =	*tva*	દ્ધ =	*ddha*	દૃ =	*drĭ*
પ્ત =	*pta*	શ્ચ =	*ścha*	લ્ય =	*lya*
પ્ન =	*pna*	શ્મ =	*śma*	જ્ય =	*jya*
પ્મ =	*pma*	શ્ર =	*śra*	લ્લ or લ્લ =	*lla*
પ્ય =	*pya*	શ્વ =	*śva*	ધ્ય =	*dhya*
પ્ર =	*pra*				

When any of these compound consonants is followed by any vowel sign, the inherent અ (*a*) is of course rejected, as in the case of simple characters.

Dv, tv, and other compounds of which *v* forms the final member, are pronounced almost like *dd, tt,* the *v* having the effect of apparently adding emphasis to the sound of the first member of the compound, but being itself very slightly pronounced.

§ 4. The Orthography of the Gujarātī language is, in some points, still unsettled, though the preparation and use in schools of Government class-books tend to fix it. In works printed a few years ago, for example, we find *vāhāñṇ* for *vahāṇ*, *hāt* for *hāth*, *bāhār* for *bahār*, etc. So also *nāhāno* is now generally written, and perhaps *always* pronounced *nāno*; and we now have *mōṭō* for *mōhōṭō*, *dahāḍo* (in Pārsī-Gujarātī pronounced *dāro*) for *dāhāḍo*. There is still great uncertainty about *i* and *u*, the long and short forms of these being often used as of equal value.

Such forms as *rahyo, kahyuñ*, etc., are pronounced almost as if written *raiyo, kaiyuñ*, owing to the feeble sound of *h*.

CHAPTER II.

Parts of Speech.—Nouns.

§ 1. There are eight parts of speech, as in English. Of these the Noun (*nām*), the Pronoun (*sarvanām*), the Adjective (*viśeshaṇ*), and the Verb (*kriyāpad*) are capable of inflection (*ākhyey*): the rest being indeclinable (*avyay*).

NOUNS (*Nām*).

Nouns are Proper (*viśeshanām*), Common (*sāmānyanām*), and Abstract (*bhāvavāchakanām*). They admit of Gender, Number, and Case.

§ 2. Gender (*Jāti*).

There are three Genders in Gujarātī; *masc.* (*narajāti*), *fem.* (*nārījāti*), and *neut.* (*nānyatar*).

The Gender of a word is determined either (1) by its meaning, or (2) by its termination.

Among names of living creatures, those clearly denoting males are *masc.*, those denoting females *fem.*, while those which are common to both sexes are generally *neuter*. E.g. *purush* a man, a male (*vir*) is *m.*: *strī* a woman is *fem.*, *māṇas* a human being (*homo*) is *neut.*: so also *chhokro* a boy, *masc.*; *chhokrī* a girl, *fem.*; *chhokruñ* a child, *neut.* (Cf. German das Kind, and our habit—not confined to bachelors—of speaking of an infant as *it.*)

The names of the days of the week, of months, of mountains, the heavenly bodies, oceans, seas, winds, divisions of a country, are *masculine.*

Names of Rivers (except e.g. *Brahmaputra, Sindhunad,* which are *m.*), the Earth, Lunar days (except *paḍavo, m.*), divisions of the day (except *pahor, m.*, a watch, *vigilia*), and the following members of the body, viz., *ānkh*, eye; *jāng*, thigh; *nas*, vein; *pānpaṇ*, eyelid; *khāndh*, shoulder; and *jībh*, tongue, are *feminine.*

Names of classes of animals, villages, cities, districts, the points of the compass, and most names of fruits, are *neuter.*

§ 3. *Gender as fixed by terminations.*

Most nouns ending in *-o* are *masculine.**

„ „ *-ī* or *-ā* are *feminine.*†

All „ „ *-uñ* are *neuter.*‡

Nouns derived from the stems of prepositional verbs in Sanskrit, as *vikār* (fr. $\sqrt{\text{kri}}$), change; *vichār* (fr. $\sqrt{\text{char}}$, to think), thought: and reduplicated onomatopoeic nouns ending in -āṭ (as *gaḍgaḍāṭ*, a rumbling), are *masculine.*

---

* Except: *juo*, f. or n., gambling; *chho* or *chhoo*, f., mortar; *dho*, m., washing.

† Except: (1) when the ī = Sk. iyam, ījam, &c.; e.g. *pāṇī*, n., water; *lohī* or *loī*, n., blood; *marī*, n., pepper; *bī*, n., seed; *ghī*, n., 'ghee,' clarified butter. (2) When the -ī is a term. denoting a calling, trade, or indicating in some way a male: e.g. Pārsī, m.; *hāthī*, m., a male elephant; *dhobī*, m., a washerman. (3) A few nouns in -ā are masc.: e.g. *ātmā*, spirit; *mahimā*, glory; *devatā*, a god, fire.

‡ Except *ghaüñ*, m., wheat.

All abstract nouns ending in *-āī, āś, -k, vaṇ, vaṭ, vaḍ, uṭ, tā ;* and Arabic or Persian words ending in *-at* or *-ās,* are *feminine.*

Most words ending in *-e, -t,* or *-s,* are also *feminine.*

All abstract nouns having the terminations *-aṇ, -āṇ, -paṇ, -maṇ, van, tva,* and most nouns ending in -ṇ,* are *neuter,* as are also names of countries ending in *-stān.*

Nouns derived from Sanskrit generally speaking preserve the gender they had in that language. Thus if we know that *ghar,* house, is the Sanskrit *griham, n.,* we at once know that *ghar* too is neuter. (But *vastu,* a thing, is *f.,* as in Hindī and Panjābī, though *n.* in Sanskrit.)

Words derived from Hindustānī, and through it from Arabic or Persian, usually retain the gender they had in Hindustānī ; as, *jamīn,* ground, *f.* (Urdu, زمین *f.*) ; *tasdī,* annoyance, *f.* (Urdu, تصدیع *f.*).

It is impossible to fix the gender of all words by any number of rules, but the apparent difficulty thus caused disappears with practice in the language.

More commonly there are two forms, one *masc.,* denoting a larger, and one *fem.,* meaning a smaller thing ; as, *chopḍo,* an account book, a large volume ; *chopḍī,* a book, a small ordinary book.

A few nouns have three forms, one of each gender ; as, *chhokro, m.,* a boy ; *chhokrī, f.,* a girl ; *chhokruñ, n.,* a child.

---

* Except, e.g. *āṇ,* 'an oath,' *f.*

§ 4. Number (*Vachan*).

In Gujarātī there are two numbers, Singular and Plural (called *ekavachan* and *bahuvachan* or *anekavachan* respectively). The plural termination is universally *-o*, though this ending is not always required to denote plurality. A few classes of nouns (see under *Declension*) undergo a slight change before taking this affix.

Some nouns, as *tal, mag, aḍad, marī*, are used only in the plural.

Such nouns of *materials* as *retī*, sand, *vāḷ*, hair, *rū*, cotton, *māṭī*, soil, earth, *dhānya*, corn; also names of metals, as *sunuñ*, gold, *rūpuñ*, silver; and moreover all abstract nouns, as *nyāy*, justice, *satyatā*, truth, *śuddhatā*, purity, *pāp*, guilt, etc., are generally used only in the singular. The plural is, however, used when either (1) different kinds of the thing specified are meant, or (2) when something special is implied. Thus *dhānyo* means 'various kinds of corn.' Cf. in English, "in *deaths* oft": *i.e.* 'in different kinds of peril of death.' Ex., "*Amārāñ pāp ghaṇāñ chhe*," 'our sins are many.' Here *pāp* is plural, as its adjj. show, though it has not assumed a plural ending.

When a cardinal numeral (*two, three*, etc.), or an adjective denoting *all* or *many*, precedes a noun, and when plurality is in this way sufficiently indicated, the noun commonly remains in the singular form, though with a plural meaning. E.g., *Tamāre gher vīs māṇas* (for *māṇaso*) *āvaśe*, 'twenty men will come to your house.' But when a noun ends in *-o, masc.*, or *-uñ, neut.*, in the singular, *it must take the plural form* in such a case.

Sometimes a noun of material has a plural with a difference of meaning: e.g. *lugḍuñ*, cloth; *lugḍāñ*, clothes, garments; *loḍhuñ*, iron; *loḍhāñ*, tools.

A noun often occurs in the plural when the meaning is singular, in order to show respect. This, however, is the case only with nouns signifying *persons*. Ex., *mārā pyārā bāp sārā chhe*, 'my dear father(s) is (are) good.' If the noun so used is feminine, its adjective is put in the plural *neuter*, as *mārāñ beheno āvyāñ hatāñ*, 'my sister(s) had come' (*vide* p. 36, § 4).

§ 5. Declension (*Rūpākhyān*).

With regard to declension, nouns in Gujarātī are divided into two classes:—(1) those that end in *-o*, masc. and *-uñ*, neut.; and (2) those that do not.

The former class have two forms, the Absolute and the Oblique. The Oblique is formed from the Absolute by changing the *-o* or *-uñ* into *-ā*; and is used before all postpositions, and also as the Vocative.

As nouns belonging to the second class *do not* end in *-o* or *-uñ*, it is evident that they *remain unchanged in the singular.*

In the plural of all nouns the Absolute and the Oblique cases are one and the same in form.

Nouns ending in *-o, masc.*, take as their plural *-ā* instead; the plural thus corresponding in form with the Oblique

Singular. To this, *-o* may be added as a further sign of plurality.

Neuters in *-uñ* change this ending in the Plural into *-āñ*, to which they *may* add *-o*.

All other nouns may have the plural of the same form as the singular. Feminines in *-ī*, however, almost always add *-o* to form the plural; and other nouns also *may* do so when any plural *sign* is required.

We have, therefore, the following scheme :—

Class I.

	Masc.		*Neut.*	
	Sing.	*Plur.*	*Sing.*	*Plur.*
Abs.	*dikr-o*	*dikrā-(o)*	*lugḍ-uñ*	*lugḍ-āñ-(o)*
Obl.	*dikr-ā*	*dikrā-(o)*	*lugḍ-ā**	*lugḍ-āñ-(o)*

Class II.

	Masc.		*Neut.*	
	Sing.	*Plur.*	*Sing.*	*Plur.*
Abs.	*purush*	*purush-(o)*	*nām*	*nām-(o)*
Obl.	*purush*	*purush-(o)*	*nām*	*nām-(o)*

Feminine.

	Sing.	*Plur.*
Abs.	*dikrī*	*dikrī-o*
Obl.	*dikrī*	*dikrī-o*

---

* Some writers prefer to write the *obl. neut.* with a nasal, e.g. *lugḍāñ*, both in nouns and adjectives, but it seems best not to do so.

Instead of the *cases** of the Sanskrit, Gujarātī expresses the relation of the nouns to the other words in a sentence by certain small words corresponding to our English prepositions. The only difference is that (1) these words *follow* instead of preceding the nouns which they govern, and are hence styled *post*positions: and (2) that they are *united* in writing to their nouns, forming one word with them. The postpositions are attached to the *oblique* form of the noun. Those most commonly used are:—

ne, to (also expresses the direct object).
e, by, at. *no, nī, nuñ*, of. *māñ*, in.
thakī, vatī, or *thī*, from, with (instrument).

In Nouns of Class I., the *-ā* of the Oblique form is usually omitted before the addition of *-ē*: we have therefore both *dikrā-e* and *dikre* to mean 'by a son.' With this class of nouns, *-e* means only 'by,' denoting the Agent: but with nouns of Class II. it also means 'at,' and in this case may be compounded with *thī*, as *niśālethī*.

The termination *-no-nī-nuñ*,† agrees in number, gender

* The native Grammars conform to the Sanskrit system and arrange the nouns and these postpositions into seven (or in some books *eight*) cases (*vibhaktī*). This is, however, alien to the spirit of the Gujarātī, quite as much as a similar scheme would be to that of the English language. It has, nevertheless, the advantage (?) of making difficult what is easy.

† When a postposition beginning with a consonant is attached to a noun ending in one, the two consonants *do not* coalesce to form a compound letter. This is because, according to *theory*, the inherent vowel *-a* follows the last consonant of the noun. Thus *dev*, a god, is

and case with the *noun following*, really turning its own noun into an adjective; as, *ā māṇas*nā *dikrāne*, 'to this man's son;' *e rājānī dikrī*, 'that king's daughter.' (Vide *Adjectives.*)

More than one postposition may be attached at the same time to a noun; as, *niśāl*, 'a school;' *niśālethī* or *niśālmāñthī*, '*from in* the school' or 'from at school;' *gharmāñnī chhokrī*, 'the girl *of in* the house,' *i.e.* 'who is in the house.'

The Absolute form may be used as the *object* of a verb, and very commonly is so when the noun denotes a thing without life. The Oblique with *-ne* more commonly expresses the object when it is a noun denoting a living being, or when it is desired to *emphasize* the object.

The Absolute is sometimes used instead of the *obl.* with a preposition to denote *point of time*; as, *te* dahāḍo *mārī dikrī gaī*, 'that day my daughter went.'

It is also used to express *measure*, where we in English use 'of'; as, *traṇ loṭā* pāṇī *āpo*, 'Give three vessels *of* water.' (Cf. German Ein Glas Wein, etc.)

---

supposed to end in *a* (and to be *deva*). But as this inherent vowel in such instances is never heard, it would merely mislead the learner to write *devane* and expect him to pronounce it *devne*.

CHAPTER III.

The Adjective (*Viśeshaṇ*).

In Gujarātī, adjectives precede the nouns which they qualify.

§ 1. Adjectives are of two kinds: (1) Declinable (*vikārī*), and (2) Indeclinable (*avikārī*). To the former class belong all adjectives which have the termination *-uñ* in the *neut.* absolute. The *masc.* abs. of these ends in *-o*, and the *fem.* abs. in *-ī*, as *rāt-o, -ī, -uñ.* These are declined precisely on the model of *chhokro, chhokrī, chhokruñ, i.e.* the *m.* as *dikro,* the *f.* as *dikrī,* and the *n.* as *lugḍuñ.*

When the adjective is declinable, the noun which it qualifies (called its *viśeshya*) does not necessarily assume the *-o* of the plural *if* it belong to Class II. of nouns, the plurality being sufficiently indicated by the adj., as *ghaṇāñ ghar* or *ghaṇāñ gharo,* 'many houses.'

Adjectives that do not end in *-uñ* in the neut. abs. sing. remain unaltered when affixed to a noun, as *lāl, sufed.*

§ 2. When declinable, the adj. agrees with its noun in gender, number and case; but the postpositions are *not* affixed to adjectives when they qualify nouns *expressed.**

* This shows that these postpositions are *not* in Gujarātī *case-endings*, otherwise they would be affixed to adjectives too, as the case-endings are in Sanskrit, Latin and Greek. The only exception to this rule is in the case of the postposition *-e*, in certain instances. (*Vide* Cap. VI. ii. § 6, nos. (3) and (4), pp. 83 and 84.)

If, however, the noun is *understood*, the adj. is used as a noun, and takes the postpositions accordingly.

The plural term. *-o* is *not* generally added to plural adjectives when followed by plural nouns; but *may* be added to them when the noun is feminine, e.g. *nānī dikrīo* or *nānīō dikrīo*, 'little daughters.'

A noun with the affixes *-no*, m., *-nī*, f., *-nuñ*, n., when followed by another noun, practically becomes a declinable adjective and is treated as such : as, *ā chhokrānuñ pustak*, 'this boy's book;' *ā chhokrānā pustak māñ*, 'in this boy's book.' *Te dungrone raste āvyo*, 'he came by way of the mountains.' Here *ne* does not mean 'to,' but is formed from *-no*, just as *chhokre* is from *chhokro*, and agrees with *raste*. (*Vide* note on preceding page.)

When one adj. qualifies two nouns of different genders, it is put in the *neuter plural*; as, *bhalāñ mā pāp*, 'good parents.' This is so when the adj. is the predicate also, as *tamārā bhāī tathā tamārī beheno* ghaṇāñ *chhe*, 'your brothers and your sisters are numerous.'

§ 3. For the sake of clearness we add an example of (1) a declinable, and (2) an indeclinable adj. attached to a noun with postpositions affixed :—

(1) *Declinable.*

Singular.

Abs.	*moṭo menḍho*	a big ram.
Obl.	*moṭā menḍhā*	,,
	moṭā menḍhāne . . .	to ,,
	etc.	
	moṭā menḍhe	by ,,

Plural.

Abs.	*moṭā menḍhāo* . . .	big rams.
Obl.	*moṭā menḍhāo* . . .	„
	moṭā menḍhāone . .	to „
	etc.	
	moṭā menḍhāoe . . .	by „

(2) *Indeclinable.*

Singular.

Abs. and Obl.	*sufed ghar*	a white house.
	sufed ghare	at „
	sufed gharthī . . .	from „

Plural.

Abs. and Obl.	*sufed ghar(o)* . . .	white houses.
	sufed gharomāñ .	in „
	sufed gharothī . .	from „

§ 4. When an adjective qualifies a fem. noun plural, which denotes a *person* or *persons,* the adj. is generally put in the NEUTER *plural* to imply respect; as, *marāñ mā sārāñ chhe,* 'my mother is good.' (Here *mā* is in the 'plural of respect.') So also in addressing females, *O mārāñ pyārāñ beheno,* 'O my dear sister' or 'sisters.'

If one adjective qualifies (not *both* but) *either* of two nouns, which follow it, and are of different genders, the adj. agrees with the noun nearest to it; as, *jo ihāñ ḍoso purush ke strī hoy,* 'if any old man or woman be here.' The same rule holds good if the adjective in such an instance be the predicate; as, *gāy ke ghoḍo* langḍo *hoy*, 'if the cow or the horse be lame.'

When a declinable adj. is used as an adverb to qualify another adj. attached to a noun, it agrees with the noun in gender, number and case; as, *Ā ghoḍo* ghaṇo *rāto* (or *lāl*) *chhe*, 'this horse is *very* red.'

When a declinable adj. is used adverbially to qualify a verb, it agrees with the subject of the verb; as, *te sipāī* dhīmo *hinto hato*, 'that sepoy was walking *slow*,' (i.e. *slowly*): *ā ghoḍī ghaṇī doḍī*, 'this mare ran much.'

§ 5. *Degrees of Comparison.*

No change in the form of an adjective occurs to express the Comparative and Superlative Degrees. But the positive denotes the *comparative* when it is preceded in the same sentence by a noun or pronoun with the postposition *-kartāñ* or *-thī* attached to it; e.g., *māṇas paśukartāñ buddhimān chhe*, 'a man is wiser than a beast.'

When the adj. is preceded by a word denoting *all*, to which the before-mentioned postpositions are affixed, it denotes the superlative relation; as, *Māruñ ghar badhāñthī sāruñ chhe*, 'my house is the best of all.'

§ 6. The Numeral *ek*, 'one,' is added to adjectives denoting *many*, or any definite or indefinite number, to make a slight change in their significance. In such cases the numeral may drop its vowel. Thus we have, from *ghaṇuñ*, 'many,' nom. pl. m. *ghaṇā* + *ek* = *ghaṇāek* or *ghaṇāk*, 'a good number;' fem. *ghaṇīek* or *ghaṇīk*; neut. *ghaṇāñek* or *ghaṇāñk*.

CHAPTER IV.

The Pronoun (*Sarvanām*).

§ 1. *Personal Pronouns.*

These are slightly irregular in declension, but will be easily learnt from the following tables:—

1st Person.

Sing.	*Plur.*
Huñ, I.	*Ame*, we.
mane, me, to me.	*amne*, us, to us.
meñ, or *me*, by me.	*ame*, by us.
māre (with *sāru*, &c.), (for) me.	*amāre*, (*sāru*, &c.), (for) us.
mār-o, m., —*ī*, f., —*uñ*, n., } my.	*amār-o*, m., —*ī*, f., —*uñ*, n., } our.
mārāthī, from me.	*amārāthī*, from us.
mārāmāñ, in me.	*amārāmāñ*, in us.

2nd Person.

Sing.	*Plur.*
Tuñ, thou.	*Tame*, you.
tane, thee, to thee.	*tamne*, you, to you.
teñ or *te*, by thee.	*tame*, by you.
tāre (*sāru*, &c.), (for) thee.	*tamāre* (*sāru*, &c.), (for) you.
tār-o, m., —*ī*, f., —*uñ*, n., } thy.	*tamār-o*, m., —*ī*, f., —*uñ*, n., } your.
tārāthī, from thee.	*tamārāthī*, from you.
tārāmāñ, in thee.	*tamārāmāñ*, in you.

3rd Person.

Sing.	*Plur.*
Te, he, she, it.	*Teo*, they.
tene, him, to him, &c.	*teone*, *temne*, them, to them.
teṇe, by him.	*teoe*, *temṇe*, by them.
tene (*sāru*), (for) him.	*teone*, *temne* (*sāru*), for them.
te-no, ——*nī*, ——*nuñ*, } of him, her, &c.	*teono*, &c., or *temno*, &c., } their.
tethī, *tenāthī*, from him.	*teomāñ*, *temnāmāñ*, } in them.
temāñ, *tenāmāñ*, in him.	

In the First and Second Persons there is no distinction of Gender. In the Third,* *teṇīe* is often used for the *fem.*, 'by her,' and less commonly *teṇīne* for 'to her,' and *teṇīno*, etc., for 'of her,' 'hers': the other forms, however, may be used as feminine too, and are said to be more correct.

Wherever *mă* or *mārā* occurs above, *muj* may be used instead in the 1st Person, and similarly in the 2nd Person *tuj* instead of *ta* or *tārā*; but these forms are not used in writing and are not considered so correct.

In the Plural, we may have *amo* instead of *ame* (in the Agential *amoe*), and *tamo* (Agential *tamoe*) for *tame*.

Ame is used for *we* when the person addressed is *not* included, and may be called the *exclusive pronoun*. When the person or persons addressed *are* included in the '*we*,'

---

* The pronouns *tevaṇ*, m. and *teṇī* f., for 'he' and 'she,' are much used in Pārsī-Gujarātī. *Vide* some examples in Part V. of the subjoined Reading Lessons.

another pronoun, *Āpaṇe*, is employed instead. It is declined thus:—*Āpaṇe*, we; *āpaṇne*, us, to us; *āpaṇe*, by us, *āpaṇāthī*, from us; *āpaṇāmāñ*, in us; *āpaṇo*, *-ī*, *-ūñ*, our (poetically *āpaḍo*, *-ī*, *-uñ*).

§ 2. *Honorific Pronoun.*

Āp is used sometimes in addressing a superior, *never* as in Urdū in speaking to an equal. It is declined as if it were a noun, the postpositions being added quite regularly; as, *āp-no*, *-nī*, *-nuñ*, 'of your honour'; *āpthī*, 'from your honour,' etc. It is *plural*, and of the 2nd Person, (not, as in Urdū, of the 3rd).

The usual word for 'you' is *tame*, which is used just as the corresponding English word. *Tuñ* is rarely used but in addressing children, except in the villages, where the country-people address one another by this pronoun.

§ 3. *Reflexive Pronoun.*

The Reflexive Pronoun is *pote*, Obl. *potā*. It is used for all three genders and both numbers, and signifies 'himself,' 'herself,' 'itself,' 'themselves,' being of the third person. The Agential corresponds with the Absolute in form, and for *potāthī*, 'from himself,' &c., we may also have *potānāthī*, with the same meaning. A reduplicated form, *potpote*, is also used with a distributive sense, 'each himself.' E.g. while *te logo potāne gher gayā* means 'those people went to their own home,'—implying that they had one home in common,—*te logo potpotānē gher gayā* would mean 'those people went each to his own home.' (*Gher* is for *ghare,* i.e. *ghar* + the termination *-e* meaning *in* or *at,*—here *to.*) Another reflexive pronoun is *paṇḍe,* 'himself,' 'self'; as, *Rājā paṇḍe bhaṇelo hato.*

It is necessary to call attention to the fact that *pote,* in the possessive form *potāno, potānī, potānuñ,* is not used with regard to the 1st, and hardly ever with reference to the 2nd person. Therefore, instead of saying, as in Urdū, *maiñ* apnī *kitāb paṛhtā hūñ,* in Gujarātī we say *huñ* mārī *chopḍī vāñchuñ chhuñ.* But we say:—*Huñ pote chālyo,* '*I myself* went;' *tuñ pote jośe,* 'thou thyself shalt see;' *teo pote āvyā,* 'they themselves came:' also, *Huñ potāno nyāya karto nathī,* 'I judge not myself,' because *nyāya karvo* is a verb.

Instead of *potpotāno, sau sauno* (*sau* = 'each') may be used; as, *tame sau saunī jagāe beśī jāo,* 'go ye and sit down, each in his own place.'

§ 4. *Interrogative Pronouns.*

1. *Koṇ,* 'who?' is of both numbers and is of all three genders. In its declension it has three forms for the Oblique, viz. *koṇa, ko* and *ke,* otherwise it is regular, being declined like a noun of Class II. by the addition of the proper postpositions, as *koṇane, kone,* or *kene,* 'whom?' 'to whom?' Like other pronouns it allows the possessive to be used, instead of the simple oblique, before *-māñ* and *-thī,* as *koṇthī, konāthī,* or *kenāthī,* 'from whom?'

2. *Kayo,* m., *kaī,* f., *kayuñ,* n., = 'which?' (Urdū

کِرنسا). It is declined like an ordinary adjective of its class. Another form is *kiyo, keī, kiyuñ*.

3. *Śo*, m., *śī*, f., *śuñ*, n., = 'What?' is declined regularly, except that (1) in the sing. it has two forms of the oblique, *śā* and *śe*, m. and n.; and (2) that its agential form, after the manner of the personal pronouns, prefixes *ṇ* to the postposition *-e*, becoming *śāṇe* or *śeṇe*, 'by what?' The neut. is used as a pronoun, 'What?'; the word is rather an interrogative adjective than a pronoun in other respects; as, *teo* śī *rīte e kām kare chhe*, 'in *what* manner do they do this work?' (The *ś* in this word is almost universally pronounced as if it were *s*.)

§ 5. *Relatives and Indefinites.*

1. *Koī*, 'any one,' 'some one,' with a negative 'no one,' is also a relative adj. When a pronoun it takes the affixed postpositions. The Oblique is the same as the Absolute form; e.g., *ā roṭlī koīṇe āpo*, 'give this bread to some one.' When *koī* may mean either a male or a female, its verb is generally *neuter*; as, *koī jāṇtuñ nahatuñ*, 'no one knew.'

2. *Je*, 'who,' 'which,' 'that,' is of all three genders. It is declined on the model of *Te*. Whenever *je* occurs in a sentence, if it is not preceded by *te*, the latter must follow it; as, *Rājāe tene mārī nāñkhyo, eṭle je sipāī meñ kāle dīṭho, tene*, 'The king killed him, *i.e.* the soldier whom I saw yesterday, *him*.'

'Whoever,' 'whosoever,' 'whatever,' is expressed by the reduplication of *je*, and consequently of the accompanying *te*; as, Je je *ṭhekāṇe dhartī rasāḷ dīṭhī*, te te *ṭhekāṇe teo vaśyā*, '*Wherever* they found the ground fertile, *there* they dwelt.'

Kaīñ or *kāīñ* is the indefinite pronoun denoting an *uncertain amount* or *quantity* = 'some' (Urdū کچھ); as, 'Give me some tea,' *mane kaīñ chā āpo*. It is therefore generally used for inanimate things.

§ 6. *Demonstratives.*

These are more properly adjectives than pronouns, but are entered here because, when used apart from nouns, they become pronouns. The principal are: *Ā*, this; *E*, that; *Te*, that; *Pelo, -ī, -uñ*, that; *Olyo, -ī, -uñ*, that; *Falāṇo, -ī, -uñ*, a certain. The last three are declined as regular declinable adjectives, the first three when used as demonstratives are indeclinable.

From *Ā, E, Te, Je, Ke*, a number of very useful demonstrative, relative, and interrogative adjectives are formed, as will be seen from the appended list:—

Ā, this.	*E*, that.
āvo, such as this.	*evo*, such as that.
āṭlo, as much as this.	*eṭlo*, as much as that.
āvaḍo, as big as this.	*evaḍo*, as big as that.

Te, that.

tevo, such as that.
teṭlo, as much as that.
tevaḍo, as big as that.

The forms from *Je* and *Ke* are produced by putting *J* and *K* respectively in place of *T* in the last column. These words are all regularly declined; as, *kevo*, m.; *kevī*, f.; *kevuñ*, n. If united to a preceding noun they require the *oblique* form of it; as, *tobrā jevuñ moñ*, 'a somewhat angry face,' 'puffed cheeks.'

The enclitic *j* is often attached to pronouns (as also to nouns) in Gujarātī to add emphasis, being used just as is -*tza* (च) in Marāṭhī and *hī* in Urdū. So we have *tej* = 'he indeed,' 'that very;' *tevoj*, 'just such as that,' &c. If a postposition is added to the noun, *j* follows the postposition; as, *ā niśalmāñj*, 'in this very school.'

CHAPTER V.

The Verb (*Kriyāpad*).

The Gujarātī Verb is conjugated very simply, there being only one conjugation which is employed for all verbs. A few verbs (*vide* § 11), form their past tense irregularly, but when formed it is conjugated just as in all other verbs in the language.

§ 1. The Stem (*mūḷ*) of the Verb is its simplest form, and is used as the 2nd Sing. Imperat. also, e.g. *utar*, 'descend.'

The Infinitive is formed by affixing *-vuñ* to the stem; as, *utar-vuñ*, 'to descend.' This is the part of the verb given in dictionaries.

The Present Part. changes the *-vuñ* of the Infinitive into *-to*, *-tī*, *-tuñ*, (e.g. *utar-to*), and is declined as a regular adjective.

The Preterite is formed by adding *-yo*, *-ī*, *-yuñ* to the stem for *m.*, *f.* and *n.*, respectively; as, *utar-yo*, 'he descended.'

The Aorist is formed by adding to the stem the remains of the original Sanskṛit pronominal terminations. In Gujarātī these are:—

	Sing.	*Plur.*
1st,	*-uñ*	*-īe*
2nd,	*-e*	*-o*
3rd,	*-e*	*-e*

The Future is formed by adding to the stem the following affixes:—

	Sing	*Plur.*
1st,	-*īś*.	-*īśuñ* (also -*aśuñ* and -*iśuñ*).
2nd,	-*śe* (vulg. -*je*).	-*śo* (vulg. *jo*).
3rd,	-*śe*.	-*śe*.

There are three Primary Tenses—the Aorist, the Future, and the Preterite. From the first and last of these, and from the declinable participles, compound tenses are formed with the assistance of the auxiliary Verbs, $\sqrt{\textit{chha}}$ and *hovuñ*, 'to be.'

The Passive Voice is formed from the stem by adding -*ā* to it, and then affixing the terminations already mentioned; as, *lakh*, 'write thou;' *lakh-ā-vuñ*, 'to be written;' *lakhāśe*, 'it will be written,' &c.

If the stem have an *intransitive* signification, three or more forms may spring from it; as, *marvuñ*, 'to die;' *mārvuñ*, 'to strike;' *marāvuñ*, 'to quarrel;' *marāvavuñ*, 'to cause to be beaten:' so also *karvuñ*, 'to do,' 'to make;' *karāvuñ*, 'to be done;' *karāvavuñ*, 'to cause to be done,' although *karvuñ* is *transitive*.

The two great classes of Verbs are:—(1) Transitives (*Sakarmak*), and (2) Intransitives (*Akarmak*). It is only in the *use* of the Preterite, and of the tenses derived from it, that any difference between the two classes is noticeable as far as conjugation is concerned. We take the latter first:—

§ 2. *Intransitive Verb. Active Voice* (Karmak Bhed *or* Mūḷ Bhed).

I. *Simple Tenses.* — (1) *Primary.*

(*a*) Aorist (*Aniyamitavartmānkāḷ*).

Sing.	*Plur.*
1st Pers., *huñ utar-uñ*, I may descend.	1st Pers., *ame utar-īe*, we may descend.
2nd Pers., *tuñ utar-e*, thou mayest descend.	2nd Pers., *tame utar-o*, you may descend.
3rd Pers., *te utar-e*, he may descend.	3rd Pers., *teo utar-e*, they may descend.

(*b*) Imperative.

2nd Pers., Sing., *utar*; Plur., *utaro*.

(*c*) Future (*Bhavishyakāḷ*).

Sing.	*Plur.*
1st Pers., *huñ utar-īś*, I shall descend.	1st Pers., *ame utar-īśuñ*, we shall descend.
2nd Pers., *tuñ utar-śe*, thou wilt descend.	2nd Pers., *tame utar-śo*, you will descend.
3rd Pers., *te utar-śe*, he will descend.	3rd Pers., *teo utar-śe*, they will descend.

(*d*) Preterite (*Bhūtakāḷ*).—1st, 2nd, 3rd Person.

Sing.	*Plur.*
m., *utar-yo*,* (I, thou, he) descended.	m., *utar-yā*, we, &c.
f., *utar-ī*, (I, thou, she) descended.	f., *utar-ī*, we, &c.
n., *utar-yuñ*, (I, thou, it) descended.	n., *utar-yāñ*, we, &c.

To these forms the pronouns are prefixed, as *huñ*, *tuñ*, *te utaryo*, if the subject is masc.; *huñ*, *tuñ*, *te utarī*, if fem.; and *huñ*, *tuñ*, *te utaryuñ*, if it is neuter.

§ 3. I. *Simple Tenses*.—(2) *Secondary*.

(*a*) Past Subjunctive (*Sanketabhūtakāḷ*).

This has only *one* form for both numbers and all three persons.

1st, 2nd, and 3rd Person.

Sing.	*Plur.*
utar-at, (If I, &c.) were *or* would be.	*utar-at*, (If we, &c.), were *or* would be.

(For the use of this tense, see examples under the Past Subj. of the auxiliary *hovuñ*.)

---

* Sometimes the *y* of the preterite is omitted in the old style of writing, and we have *utaro*, *gao*, *karo*, for *utaryo*, *gayo*, *karyo*, &c. At others *e* is put instead of *y*, as *āveo* for *āvyo*.

(*b*) Past Indefinite (*Aniyamitabhūtakāḷ*).

This is the Present Participle used as a finite Verb. It therefore agrees in *gender* also with its subject.

1st, 2nd and 3rd Person.

Sing.	*Plur.*
m., *utar-to*, I, thou, he, used to descend.	*utar-tā*, we, you, they, used to descend.
f., *utar-tī*, I, thou, she, &c.	*utar-tī*, we, you, they, &c.
n., *utar-tuñ*, I, thou, it, &c.	*utar-tuñ*, we, you, they, &c.

The pronouns are prefixed quite regularly to these tenses.

(*c*) The Precative.

This is the same as the *Aorist*, except that in the 3rd Pers. Sing. and Pl. the termination *-o* is used instead of *-e*; as, *te*, *teo utaro*, 'may he, they descend.' Ex., *Kirpā tamāre sāthe* thāo (fr. *thavuñ*), 'Grace *be* with you.' It is especially used in blessing or cursing. Another Precative (Future Precative) is formed by changing the *-śe* of the 3rd Sing. and 3rd Plur. into *-jo*; as, *tamāruñ bhaluñ* thajo, 'may you good *be*,' i.e. 'may you be blessed;' *Te śrāpit thāo*, 'may he be cursed.'

Hence we have: *te utar-jo*, sing.; *teo utar-jo*, plur.

(*d*) Future Imperative.

Sing.	*Plur.*
2nd Pers., *tuñ utar-je*, thou shalt descend.	*tame utar-jo*, you shall descend.

§ 4. II. *Compound Tenses.*

These are formed by combining with the Aorist, the Preterite, and the declinable Participles and Gerund (or Gerundive), certain tenses of the substantive verb. We therefore give here (1) the Participles and Gerund (Gerundive, Infinitive, &c.) of the ordinary verb, and (2) the conjugation of the Auxiliary.

(*a*) Participles, &c. (*Kridant*).

Infinitive, *utar-vuñ.*	Gerundive, *utar-vo, -vī, -vuñ.*
Pres. Participle, *utar-to, -tī, -tuñ.*	Past Participle, *utar-yo, -ī, -yuñ.*
Connective Participle, *utar-īne.*	Plup. Participle, *uṭar-elo, -ī, -uñ,* (also *utarel,* indecl.).

Agential (declinable), *utar-nār-o, -ī, -uñ;* (indecl.) *utarnār,* 'a descender.'

The Infinitive when declined is treated like a neuter noun ending in *-uñ,* and makes its *oblique* in *-vā;* as, *te* vāñchvāne *āvyo,* or *vāñchvā āvyo,* 'he came to read.'

The Gerundive is an adjective, declined quite regularly, and agrees with the noun it qualifies; as, *māre ā chopḍī vāñchvī,* 'hic liber mihi *est* legendus,' 'I must read this book;' *teṇe e kām karvuñ,* 'illi id opus faciendum,' 'he must do that work.' The verb 'to be' is generally omitted in such sentences.

When used impersonally the Gerundive is neuter; as, *tāre ramvuñ,* 'thou must play.' It is then a kind (often a polite kind) of imperative.

The Present, Past, and Pluperfect Participles are declinable Adjectives. The declinable form of the Agential Participle is also regular. The indeclinable Agential Participle is generally a noun.

The Connective Participle is like our Perfect Participle Active, as *utarīne*, 'having descended.' It is indeclinable, and has a shorter form (*utarī*) also.

The Neuter Plural of the Present Participle is often counted as an independent Participle. It is used to denote 'in the state of,' as *utartāñ*, 'in the act of descending.'* This form of the participle is also used in such constructions as the following:—*Teṇe chopḍī vāñchtāñ sikhvuñ*, 'he must learn to read a book.'

§ 5. (*b*) *The Substantive* (*Auxiliary*) *Verb.*

(1) Root $\sqrt{\textit{chha}}$. Present Tense.

	Sing.	*Plur.*
1st Pers.,	*huñ chhuñ*, I am.	*ame chhīe* (vulg. *chhaiye*), we are.
2nd Pers.,	*tuñ chhe*, thou art.	*tame chho*, you are.
3rd Pers.,	*te chhe*, he is.	*teo chhe*, they are.

(The negative of this is '*nathī*,' which is used for all three persons and both numbers.)

Pres. Part. Neut. Plur. *chhatāñ*, being. Inf. *caret*.

---

* Equivalent to *utarte hūe*, in Urdū.

(2) Root $\sqrt{ho}$, 'to be' or 'to become.'

Aorist.

Sing.	*Plur.*
1st Pers., *huñ houñ*, I may be.	*ame hoīe*, we may be.
2nd Pers., *tuñ hoy*,* thou may'st be.	*tame ho*, you may be.
3rd Pers., *te hoy*, he may be.	*teo hoy*, they may be.

Present.

The present is formed by adding the present of $\sqrt{chha}$ to the above; as, *huñ houñ chhuñ*, 'I am being,' 'I am becoming,' &c. The negative is *huñ hoto nathī*, &c.

Infinitive, *hovuñ*.	Gerundive, *hov-o, -ī, -uñ*.
Pres. Part., *hot-o, -ī, -uñ*.	(Past Part., *hav-o, -ī, -uñ*.)
Connective Part., *hoīne*.	Imper., 2nd sing. and pl., *ho*.

Agent. Part, decl., *honāro, -ī, -uñ;* indecl., *honār*.

Precative Future, *hojo*.

Fut. Imperative, *tuñ hoje; tame hojo*.

Future.

Sing.	*Plur.*
1st Pers., *haīś, hoīś*, I shall be, &c.	*ame haīśuñ, hoīśuñ*.
2nd Pers., *tuñ haśe, hośe, haīś, hoīś*, (*hoje*).	*tame haśo, hośo*, (*hojo*).
3rd Pers., *te haśe, hośe*.	*teo haśe, hośe*.

The forms in *j* are vulgar, and not used in written composition.

---

* In all verbs of which the stem ends in a *vowel*, the termination *y* takes the place of *-e* wherever the latter would otherwise occur, just as is the case in Hindī.

Past.—1st, 2nd and 3rd Person.

Sing.	*Plur.*	
m., *hato* (*havo*, vulgar).	*hatā* (*havā*, vulgar)	we were, &c.
f., *hatī* (*havī* „).	*hatī* (*havī* „)	
n., *hatuñ* (*havuñ* „).	*hatāñ* (*havuñ* „)	

When the negative *na* is prefixed, this tense becomes *nahoto*, &c.

Past Subjunctive.

In all persons and both numbers, . . . *hot* (vulg. *hat*). '(If) I, &c., were:' e.g., *Jo huñ sāro hot, to mārā mittro paṇ bhulā hot,* 'If I were good, my friends would be good also;' *Jo tame āndhlā hot, to tamne pāp na hot,* 'If ye were blind, ye had not had sin.'

---

§ 6. *Compound Tenses of* Utarvuñ, '*To descend.*'

Indicative Mood (Niśchayārth).

(*a*) Present Tense (*Vartmān*).

Formed by adding the present of √*chha* to the aorist.

Sing.	*Plur.*
1st Pers., *huñ utar-uñ chh-uñ* I am descending.	*ame utar-īe chh-īe*, we are descending.
2nd Pers., *tuñ utar-e chh-e*, thou art descending.	*tame utar-o chh-o*, you are descending.
3rd Pers., *te utar-e chh-e*, he is descending.	*teo utar-e chh-e*, they are descending.

This tense has also the meaning, 'I descend,' &c. In

the *Negative*, the Present Participle with *nathī* is used instead of the tense as above given; as, *huñ utarto* (*-tī*, *tuñ*) *nathī*, 'I do not descend.'

(*b*) Imperfect (*Vartmān Bhūt*).

Formed by adding the Past Tense of *hovuñ* to the Present Participle.

1st, 2nd, and 3rd Person.

Sing.	*Plur.*
m., *huñ*, &c., *utarto hato*.	*ame*, &c., *utartā hatā*.
f., *huñ*, &c., *utartī hatī*.	*ame*, &c., *utartī hatī*.
n., *huñ*, &c., *utartuñ hatuñ*.	*ame*, &c., *utartāñ hatāñ*.

Meaning—'I, &c., was descending.'

Negative—*huñ*, &c., *utarto nahoto*, 'I was not descending.'

(*c*) Future Gerundial (*Bhavishyavartmān*).

Formed from the Gerund or Infinitive by adding the postposition *-no*, m.; *-nī*, f.; *-nuñ*, n., to the oblique form, and appending the present of $\sqrt{chha}$.

Sing.	*Plur.*
1st Pers., m., *huñ utarvāno chhuñ*, I am about to descend.	*ame utarvānā chhīe*, &c.

The rest of the persons are formed quite regularly, in a similar way.

(*d*) Past Gerundial (*Bhavishyabhūt*).

Formed by adding the past tense of *hovuñ* to the possessive form of the gerund, as in the preceding tense.

1st, 2nd, and 3rd Person.

Sing.	*Plur.*
m., *huñ utarvāno hato*, &c.	*ame utarvānā hatā*, &c.

Meaning—'I was about to descend,' &c.

(*e*) Present Perfect (*Bhūtavartmān*).

Formed by adding the present of $\sqrt{\textit{chha}}$ to the Past Participle.

Sing.	*Plur.*
1st Pers., m., *huñ utaryo chhuñ*, I have descended.	*ame utaryā chhīe*, we have descended.
2nd Pers., m., *tuñ utaryo chhe*, thou hast descended.	*tame utaryā chho*, you have descended.
3rd Pers., m., *te utaryo chhe*, he has descended.	*teo utaryā chhe*, they have descended.

For the *fem.* and *neut.*, the *utaryo* becomes *utarī* and *utaryuñ* respectively in the Sing., and *utarī* and *utaryāñ* in the Plur. (With this and the Pluperfect tense compare the French 'Je *suis* allé,' and our 'I *am* come,' for 'I *have* come.')

(*f*) Pluperfect (*Dvitvabhūt*).

Formed by adding the Past of *hovuñ* to the Past Participle.

1st, 2nd and 3rd Person.

Sing.	*Plur.*
m., *hun*, &c., *utaryo hato.*	*ame*, &c., *utaryā hatā.*
f., *huñ*, &c., *utarī hatī.*	*ame*, &c., *utarī hatī.*
n., *huñ*, &c., *utaryuñ hatuñ.*	*ame*, &c., *utaryāñ hatāñ.*

Meaning—'I had descended,' &c.

(*g*) Second Perfect (*Viśeshabhūtavartmān*).

Formed from the Pluperfect Participle by adding the Present of √*chha.*

Sing.	*Plur.*
1st Pers., m., *huñ utarelo chhuñ.*	*ame utarelā chhīe.*
2nd Pers., m., *tuñ utarelo chhe.*	*tame utarelā chho.*
3rd Pers., m., *te utarelo chhe.*	*teo utarelā chhe.*

The Fem. and Neut. are formed by changing the terminations of the Participle as above in (*e*).

Meaning—'I am in-the-state-of-having-descended;' *i.e.*, 'I have descended,' &c.

(*h*) Second Pluperfect Tense (*Dritvaviśeshabhūtavartmān**).

Formed as the Second Perfect, substituting *hato*, &c., for *chhuñ*.

* When expressing in language strong, if not courteous, his admiration (?) for these ponderous names (the analysis of which is, however, easy), I trust the student will remember that *I* am not guilty of inventing them. They may help him if he is reading with a native Paṇḍit.

1st, 2nd and 3rd Person.

Sing.	*Plur.*
m., *huñ*, &c., *utarelo hato.*	*ame*, &c., *utarelā hatā.*

The Fem. and Neut. are formed quite regularly, by the usual change of gender.

Meaning—'I had descended,' &c.

---

§ 7. *Subjunctive Mood* (Sanśayārth *or* Sanketārth).

For each of the above eight Compound Tenses in the Indicative, there is a corresponding tense in the Subjunctive. The formation of these is very easily understood. It consists in putting the Aorist of *hovuñ* wherever the Present of √*chha* occurs in these Indicative tenses (except in the Present, which see), and the Past Subjunctive of *hovuñ* wherever *hato* is found in them. We have therefore:—

1. Present . . . . *Hun* utarto *houñ*, &c.
2. Imperfect . . . . „ „ *hot*, &c.
3. Future Gerundial . . „ utarvāno *houñ*, &c.
4. Past Gerundial . . . . „ „ *hot*, &c.
5. Present Perfect . . . . „ utaryo *houñ*, &c.
6 Pluperfect . . . . „ „ *hot*, &c.
7. Second Perfect . . . . „ utarelo *houñ*, &c.
8. Second Pluperfect . . „ „ *hot*, &c.

---

§ 8. *Use of Tenses.*

The use of most of the Tenses is quite evident from their

meanings, as already given. A few, however, are used in more than one acceptation, and need perhaps a few words of explanation.

1. The *Aorist* is so called because of its indefiniteness. It is very much more 'unlimited' in its use than is the tense in Greek, from whence the English word is derived. Generally, the Gujarātī Aorist means *may*, as *Huñ āvuñ*, 'I may come.' It also asks a question, in which we would translate it by the *form* of the English Future, as *Huñ nikluñ śuñ?* 'Shall I' *or* 'May I go out?' It moreover implies a wish; and, when (as frequently) followed by *to* or some similar particle, may be translated by the subjunctive with *if*; as, *Te jāy, to huñ āvīś*, 'If he go, then I shall come.'

But it very frequently, especially in the historical style, has a *past* sense, generally meaning 'used to,' and denoting a state of things continuing for some time, or more frequently a regularly repeated action. In this case some past tense *before* the Aorist shows that it has this sense. *E.g.*, in the following sentences, in which the Past Indefinites, which precede, fix the meaning of the Aorists:—

E adhikārīo rājāne sārū kheḍutpāsethī vaje vasūl kartā, *vepārīpāsethī mālupar jakāt* letā . . . . *Rājā sarvupar uparīpaṇuñ rākhīne prajāno insāf* kare; *khūn* kare, *tene śūlīe* chaḍāve; *ane chornāñ kānḍāñ* kāpe, *paṇ halkā gunhā karnārpāsethī danḍaj* le. 'These officials *used to collect*, on the king's behalf, the revenue from the husbandmen, *exact* custom-dues from the traders . . . . The king, retaining the oversight over all, *did* (*i.e.* used to do) justice towards his subjects; (if any one) committed murder, he *would hang* him on a stake (impale him), and he *used to cut off* the hands of thieves at the wrist; moreover, he *exacted* a fine from those who committed slight offences.'

2. The Past Indefinite might also be called the Continuative, since its general use is to show a long continued action. This also is well exemplified in the above sentence.

3. The Neut. sing. of the Past and Pluperfect Participles are often used as nouns; as, *tāruñ kaheluñ* (or *kahyuñ*) *sāruñ chhe*, 'what thou hast said (thy saying) is good.'

4. The Connective Participle is like our Part. in 'having;' as, *Rājā tene joīne niklī gayo*, 'the king, having seen him, went out.' When two finite verbs are in English connected by 'and,' the first of them is often expressed by this Participle in Gujarātī, the conjunction being omitted.

§ 9. *Negatives attached to Verbs.*

It is convenient to treat these Adverbs here. The Negatives in Gujarātī are—*Māñ*, *nā*, *na*, *nathī*, and *nahi* (also written *nahīñ*).

Māñ or *mā* is *prohibitive*, and is used *after* the Imperative Present and Future; as, *Bīho mā*, 'fear ye not.'

Nā = our 'No,' in answering a question in the negative. (But *nā kehevī* is 'to refuse.')

Na is prefixed to the Aorist and 2nd Future; also to the Past Tense of *hovuñ*, in which case the two words are written as one, and *na* + *hato* becomes *nahoto* very frequently, though not necessarily.

Nathī is used as the negative of *chhuñ, chhe,* &c. It is used only with the Pres. and Pres. Perf., and then changes the verb in the way shown in the annexed examples: e.g., *te vāñche chhe,* 'he is reading;' *te vāñchto nathī,* 'he is not reading:' *tame chālyā chho,* 'you have walked;' *tame chālyā nathī,* 'you have not walked.'

Nahi may be used everywhere except in the Present and Present Perfect tenses, and generally follows the verb. When prefixed it gives particular emphasis, and often gives to the Aorist a future negative signification. In the same way *nathī* may be prefixed in the Present and Present Perfect tenses to strengthen the negative; as, *huñ ā vinantī karuñ chhuñ,* 'I make this request;' *huñ ā vinantī nathī karto,* 'I do *not* make this request;' *Koīno vināś nathī thayo,* 'No one *at all* has perished.'

§ 10. *The Transitive Verb.*

This is conjugated exactly according to the model given under Intransitives, *except* that (with a few exceptions) *

* The principal of which are:—

Aḍvuñ, to impede.
Aḍakvuñ, to touch.
Babaḍvuñ, or *Baḍbaḍvun,* to prate.
Bhaṇvuñ, to learn.
Bhulvuñ, to forget.
Bheṭvuñ, to embrace.
Bolvuñ, to say.
Chūkvuñ, to finish.
Jītvuñ, to conquer.
Jamvuñ, to eat.
Lāvuñ, to bring.
Maḷvuñ, to get.
Pāmvuñ, to gain.
Samajvuñ, to understand.
Sīkhvuñ, to learn.
Vadvuñ, to adore.
Vaḷagvuñ, to embrace.

These verbs, though transitive, retain the Subject in the Absolute form.

the *Subject* of the verb, in the Preterite and all tenses formed from it, is put in the *Agential form, i.e.* has the postposition *-e* attached to its oblique state. In these tenses the verb agrees in *gender* and *number* with the logical *object*, and in *case* too, unless the object be governed by the postposition *-ne*.

Taking as our example, therefore, the verb *Rākhvuñ*, 'to keep,' we have in these tenses:—

(*a*) Preterite.

Sing.	*Plur.*
1st Pers., *meñ rākhyuñ*, I kept.	*ame rākhyuñ*, we kept.
2nd Pers., *teñ rākhyuñ*, thou kept.	*tame rākhyuñ*, you kept.
3rd Pers., *teṇe rākhyuñ*, he kept.	*teoe rākhyuñ*, they kept.

Example :—Teṇe nagar vasāvyuñ, 'He built a city' (*or literally*, 'He caused a city to be inhabited').

The Past Participle in Transitive Verbs has really a *Passive* signification, and we might perhaps understand the construction better if we rendered the sentence, 'The city was built by him.' But the form of this Participle, agreeing as it does with that of Intransitive Verbs, and differing from that of all formations from the Passive Stem (*vide* § 12, p. 67), as well as the fact that the *Agential* form of a noun or pronoun *cannot* be used with the passive,—all this compels us to call this and similar tenses *active.*

The Subject of the Verb in this construction is put in the *oblique* form, and has the postposition *-e* attached to it. The Object is generally (unless when at a distance from the verb) in the Absolute form if it denotes a *thing*: if it implies a *living creature*, but *not a person*, it frequently remains in the Absolute form, but not uncommonly is put in the Oblique with *-ne*: if it is the proper or common name of a *person*, the Object is usually in the Oblique form with *-ne* attached. As the postposition *-ne* also denotes the indirect object, in some sentences it occurs with both meanings.

A study of the following examples will probably make the practical application of this clear.

(1) Verb agreeing with object in gender, number and case :—

E bāīe vagaḍâmāñ dahāḍā kahāḍyā, 'That lady passed her days in the wilderness.' Here *kahāḍyā* is Absolute, *pl. m.*, to agree with *dahāḍā*.

Again :—*E nagarmāñ teṇe rājdhānī karī*, 'In that city he fixed the seat of government.' Here the verb *karī* is *f.*, to agree with the logical object *rājdhānī*, which is Abs., *sing. fem.*

(2) Verb agreeing in gender and number with the object, but *not* in *case* :—

Tene e rājāe pakaḍyo, 'That king seized him.' Here *pakaḍyo* is *masc. sing.*, to agree with *tene*, 'him,' but is in the *Absolute*, while *tene* is in the *Oblique* form with *-ne*.

Again:—*Teṇe Rāṇīne rānmāñ nasāḍī mūkī*, 'He removed

the queen into a forest.' Here the verb *mūkī* (the finite portion of the compound) is in the *fem. sing.*, agreeing with the object *Rāṇī* in this, though *not* in case, as *Rāṇi* is in the oblique with *-ne*.

(3) Verb in neuter impersonal, the object being a sentence:—

Rājāe vichāryuñ ke have to vakhat āvyo, 'The king thought that now the time was come.' Here the sentence *Have to vakhat āvyo* is the real object, and it is treated as a neuter.

(*b*) Present Perfect.

	Sing.	*Plur.*
1st Pers.,	*meñ rākhyuñ chhe*, I have kept.	*ame rākhyuñ chhe*, we have kept.
2nd Pers.,	*teñ rākhyuñ chhe*, thou hast kept.	*tame rākhyuñ chhe*, you have kept.
3rd Pers.,	*teṇe rākhyuñ chhe*, he has kept.	*teoe rākhyuñ chhe*, they have kept.

The construction is exactly similar to that just explained.

(*c*) Pluperfect.

	Sing.	*Plur.*
1st Pers.,	*meñ rākhyuñ hatuñ*, I had kept.	*ame rākhyuñ hatuñ*, we had kept.
2nd Pers.,	*teñ rākhyuñ hatuñ*, thou hadst kept.	*tame rākhyuñ hatuñ*, you had kept.
3rd Pers.,	*teṇe rākhyuñ hatuñ*, he had kept.	*teoe rākhyuñ hatuñ*, they had kept.

§ 11. *Irregular Verbs.*

The Irregular Verbs in Gujarātī are very few indeed, and the only irregularities in even these that really need attention are in the formation of the Past Participle (including the tenses formed from it). The following list contains all such verbs :—

Infinitive.	*Past Participle.*	*Pluperf. Part.*
Besvuñ, to sit . .	*beṭho, -ī, -uñ* . . .	*beṭhel-o, -ī, -uñ.*
Bīhīvuñ, to fear .	*bīny-o,-ī,-un* (& *bīdho*)	*bīnel-o, -ī, -uñ.*
Dekhvuñ, to see . .	*dīṭho*, &c.	*dīṭhelo*, &c.
Devuñ,* to give . (Conn. Part. *daīne.*)	*dīdho*, &c.	*dīdhelo*, &c.
Hovuñ, to be . . .	*hato*, &c.	
Javuñ, to go . . . (Conn. Part. *jaīne.*)	*gayo, gaī, gayuñ*† .	*gayelo*, &c.
Karvuñ, to do . .	*kīdho*, &c. (or regular)	*kīdhelo* (or reg.).
Khāvuñ, to eat . .	*khādho*, &c. . . .	*khādhelo*, &c.
Levuñ, to take . . (Conn. Part. *laīne.*)	*līdho*, &c.	*līdhelo*, &c.
Marvuñ, to die . .	*muo*, &c.	*muelo* (or reg.).
Nāsvuñ, to flee . .	*nāṭho*, &c.	*nāṭhelo*, &c.
Pesvuñ, to rush in .	*peṭho*, &c.	*peṭhelo*, &c.
Pīvuñ, to drink . .	*pīdho*, &c.	*pīdhelo*, &c.
Suvuñ, to sleep . .	*suto*, &c.	*suelo*, &c.

---

* Fut. *huñ daīś*, &c.

† But) *te* jayā *kare chhe*, 'he is accustomed to go:' see Frequentatives (p. 76, II., 1).

More trifling irregularities occur in the aorist of certain verbs, of which the stems end in vowels.

(1) If the stem end in *-ā*, the termination *-e* added after it becomes changed into *-y*; as, *thavuñ*, to become, 3rd Sing. Aor. *thāy* (for *thāe*).

(2) If the stem ends in *-e*, the *-e* when added coalesces with it, as *levuñ*, to take, 3rd Sing. Aor. *le* (for *le-e*). Before the termination *-o*, the *-e* of the stem may remain, or it may be omitted, or again, it may become *y*; as, *leo*, *lo*, or *lyo*, '(you) may take.'

(3) If the stem ends in *-ī*, the termination of the 1st Plur. Aor. loses its *ī*, and so we have *ame pīe* (for *ame pīīe*), 'we drink,' from *pīvuñ*.

(4) If the stem ends in *-o*, this vowel becomes *-u* before the terminations *-e* and *-o*; as, *jovuñ*, 'to see;' *te jue*, *tame juo* (instead of *joe* and *joo*), 'he sees,' 'you see.' *Hovuñ*, 'to be,' and *kohovuñ*, 'to be rotten,' make *hoy* and *kohoy* respectively. (The Pluperf. Part. of the latter verb is *kohelo*, &c.

The slight irregularities of the following verbs will be observed from their paradigms:—

(*a*) *Thavuñ*, 'to become.' The stem is *thā*.

Aorist.

Sing.	*Plur.*	*Future.*
1st Pers., *thauñ* or *thāuñ*	*thaīe*	*thaīś*, *thaśe*, &c.
2nd Pers., *thāy*	*thāo*	
3rd Pers., *thāy*	*thāy*	

(*b*) *Javuñ*, 'to go.' Stem, *jā*.

Aorist.

Sing.	*Plur.*	*Future.*
1st Pers., *jāuñ*	*juīe*	*jaīś, jaśe*, &c.
2nd Pers., *jāy*	*jāo*	
3rd Pers., *jāy*	*jāy*	

(*c*) The Defective *Joīe*, 'it is needful.'

Aorist, both numbers, all persons, *joīe*.
Fut. „ „ *joīśe*.
Past Subj. „ „ *joīyat*.
Pres. Part., *joīt-o, -i, -uñ*, &c.
Imperfect, *joīto hato*, &c.

The construction of sentences with this verb is as in the example, '*Māre ā chopḍī joīe*,' = 'I want this book,' *or* 'This book is needful to me.'

(*d*) *Kahevuñ* or *Kehevuñ*, &c.

Kehevuñ, 'to say;' and *Rehevuñ*, or *Rahevuñ*, 'to remain,' make in the Aorist *Kehe* and *Rehe* &c. respectively, and in the Past Part. *Kahyo* &c. and *Rahyo* &c.

It should also be noticed that, if the stem of a verb ends in *s*, this letter is changed to *ś* (સ to શ) whenever it is followed by *ī* or *y*; as, *besvuñ*, 'to sit,' Conn. Part. *beśīne*; *vasvuñ*, 'to dwell,' Past Part. *vaśyo*; *nāsvuñ*, 'to flee,' Conn. Part. *nāśīne* (though *nāsīne* is also found), &c.

§ 12. *Passive Voice* (Śakyabhed *or* Sahyabhed).

The general rule for the formation of the Passive is *to add -ā to the stem of the Active to form the Passive stem, and then attach to the new stem thus produced the same terminations as are employed in the Active.* E.g., *lakh-vuñ*, 'to write,' Active stem, *lakh*; Passive stem, *lakh-ā*: 1st Pers. Sing. Aorist Passive, *lakhāuñ*, &c.

But for the sake of euphony, and to secure ease in articulation, this rule undergoes a few slight modifications in certain instances:—

(1) If the vowel *ā* occur in the ultimate or penultimate syllable of the Active stem, this long vowel *is shortened into ă* before the addition of the Passive stem-affix *-ā*; as, *Vāpar-vuñ*, 'to use;' Passive stem, *văparā-*.

(2) If the stem of the Active end in a vowel, or in *h* preceded by a vowel, the syllable *-vā* is added, instead of merely *-ā*, to form the Passive stem; as, *pī-vuñ*, 'to drink,' stem *pī-*; Passive stem *pīvā-*. If, however, the final vowel of the Active stem be *-ā*, this is shortened (in agreement with Rule 1) before the addition of the *vā*; as, *gāvuñ*, 'to sing,' Active stem *gā*, Passive stem *găvā*.

The *logical* subject of Passive verbs, *i.e.* the doer of the action implied by them, is put in the *oblique* case followed by *-thī* (NEVER in the oblique followed by *-e*); as, *Rājāthī e kām karāyuñ*, 'that work was done by the Rājā.'

I.—*Passive of the Transitive Verb.*

Infinitive Act. *Dekhvuñ*, 'to see;' Stem, Act. *Dekh-*.

Aorist.

Sing.	*Plur.*
1st Pers., *huñ dekhāuñ*, I may seem, *or* may be seen.	*ame dekhāīe*, we may seem, *or* may be seen.
2nd Pers., *tuñ dekhāy*,* &c.	*tame dekhāo*, &c.
3rd Pers., *te dekhāy*,* &c.	*teo dekhāy*,* &c.

Present.

Sing.	*Plur.*
1st Pers., *huñ dekhāuñ chhuñ*, &c.	*ame dekhāīe chhīe*, &c.

Future.

Sing.	*Plur.*
1st Pers., *huñ dekhāīś.*	*ame dekhāīśuñ*, &c.
2nd Pers., *tuñ dekhāśe* or *dekhāīś*, &c.	

Preterite.—1st, 2nd, 3rd Pers.

Sing.	*Plur.*
M., *dekhāyo*; f., *dekhāī*; n., *dekhāyuñ*.	*dekhāyā, dekhāī, dekhāyāñ.*

---

* See above, § 5, p. 52, no. (2), and note; also p. 65, (1).

Infinitive . . . . *dekhāvuñ.*
Past Part. . . . . *dekhā-yo, -ī, -yuñ.**
Present Part. . . *dekhāt-o, -ī, uñ.*
Agential Part. . *dekhānār-o, -ī, -uñ;* and indecl., *dekhānār.*
Gerundive . . . . *dekhāv-o, -ī, -uñ.*
Pluperf. Part. . . *dekhāyel-o, -ī, -uñ* or *dekhāel-o, -ī, -uñ.*†
Connective Part. *dekhāīne, dekhāī.*

It is unnecessary to give paradigms of all the tenses at length, as their formation will now be readily understood.

Instead of the Preterite Passive, one of two circumlocutions may be used. (1) The Past Participle of the Active, followed by the Preterite of *javuñ*, 'to go;' as, *te marāyo* or *te māryo gayo*, 'he was killed' or 'struck.' (2) The Oblique Infinitive with *māñ*, followed by the Present or Past, &c., of the verb *āvavuñ*, 'to come;' as, *E vastu jovāmāñ āvī*, 'that thing was seen,'—literally, *came into seeing*. This latter construction may be used with all tenses; as, *Ā vāt kehevāmāñ āvśe*, 'this story will be told.' It is very frequently met with in Pārsī-Gujarātī.

§ 13. II. *Passive of the Intransitive Verb.*

Intransitive verbs are not unfrequently used in the

---

* Dialectically *dekhāṇuñ*. This form (m. *ṇo*, f. *ṇī*, neut. *ṇuñ*) is also used in the Preterite.

† As in the Active, the indeclinable form (*dekhāel*) is also used.

passive voice. This will not appear strange to the classical student who has, in his boyhood, had his ambition roused, let us hope, by such phrases as, "Sic *itur* ad astra." As in Latin, however, the Intransitive Verb exists in the Passive only in the *third person singular*. With this exception, the Intransitive Verb forms its Passive just as does the Transitive. *E.g.*—

(Act. Infin., *Āvavuñ*, 'to come;')
Pass. Infin., *Āvāvuñ*.

Aorist	*Āvāy.*
Present	*Āvāy chhe.*
Present Participle .	*Āvā-to, -tī, -tuñ.*
Past Participle . .	*Āvā-yo, -ī, -yuñ.*
Future	*Āvāśe.*
Pluperf. Participle .	*Āvāel-o, -ī, -uñ.*
Agent. Participle .	*Āvānār-o, -ī, -uñ*, &c., &c.

(This verb does *not* shorten the *ā* of the Active stem.)

Of course some of these tenses and forms are very rarely used. The tense of most frequent occurrence is the Preterite.

The Passive of Intransitives has generally, especially in the negative, the idea of *possibility* or the reverse; as, *mārāthī javāyuñ nahi*, 'It was not gone by me,' = 'I *could* not go.' But this meaning is also frequent with the passive of Transitives also.

Sometimes also the negative passive implies that a thing

ought not to be; as, *Evuñ kahevāy nahi,* = 'one *should* not say so.'

§ 14. *The Causative Verb* (Prekarbhed).

The Causative Verb is very common in Gujarātī, as it is in every Indian language of Sanskrit origin. Its meaning and use may be illustrated from the scanty remains in our own language of similar forms. For instance, from 'to sit,' we form the Causative 'to set,' *i.e.* 'to cause to sit;' from 'to fall,' the Causative is 'to fell,' *i.e.* 'to cause to fall;' from 'to rise,' we have the Causative 'to raise.' So in Gujarātī, from *besvuñ,* 'to sit,' comes *besāḍvuñ,* 'to cause to sit;' from *lakhvuñ,* 'to write,' we have *lakhāvavuñ,* 'to cause to write,' 'to dictate.'

The rules for the formation of the Causative *stem* (for, when the stem is known, we conjugate the verb quite regularly) are the following:—

(1) If the stem of the simple verb is *intransitive* and monosyllabic, and if its vowel is *ă,* two causatives may be formed from it: one by lengthening the *ă* into *ā*—this merely renders the verb transitive: the other by adding the termination *-āva.**

* The final *ă* is, native grammarians would say, existent at the end of the stem of the simple verb too in the infin., and before all consonantal endings except those of the Past Participle. According to them we should have *lakhavuñ, lakhato,* &c. But, while omitting the *a* in such cases, I have inserted it here, because it is *audible* between the two *v's* of the Caus. Infin.

E.g., *vaḷ-vuñ*, st. *vaḷ*, 'to turn,' *intr.*: 1st Caus. *vāḷ-vuñ*, 'to bend,' *trans.*; 2nd Caus. *vaḷāva-vuñ*, 'to cause to turn.'

If such a verb is originally *transitive*, it takes only the *second* form of the Causative; as, *lakh-vuñ*, 'to write;' *lakhāvavuñ*, 'to cause to write.'

(2) If the stem of the simple verb have in its last syllable the vowel *ā*, this is *shortened* to *a* before the causative affix, which is frequently in such cases *-āva*, but may also be *āḍ*; as, *jāṇ-vuñ*, 'to know;' *jaṇāva-vuñ*, 'to cause to know;' *chākh-vuñ*, 'to taste;' *chakhāḍ-vuñ*, 'to cause to taste.'

(3) If the stem of the simple verb has any vowel except *a* or *ā* in its last syllable, its Causative is usually formed by adding *-āḍ*, but sometimes *-varāva* or *-āva*. The first of these terminations becomes *-vāḍ* when the last *letter* of the stem is a vowel. E.g., *besvuñ*, 'to sit,' caus. *besāḍ-vuñ*; *le-vuñ*, 'to take,' caus. *levāḍ-vuñ* or *levarāva-vuñ*.*

From some causatives a second causative may be formed by reduplicating the causative ending and observing rule (2) above; as, *kar-vuñ*, 'to do,' caus. *karāva-vuñ*, 'to cause to do;' 2nd caus. *karavāva-vuñ* [i.e., *kar* + *āva*

---

* This last term. *-varāva* is really a *double* causative, *i.e.* it is composed of *-vāḍ* (with the *ḍ* changed to *r*) + the term. *-āva*, the *ā* of the former being shortened by rule (2) above. The term. *-āḍ* is the same which sometimes occurs as *-lā* in Urdu (*biṭhlānā* for *biṭhānā*), and as *-āḷ* or *-āl* in Panjābī (*biṭhāḷnā*).

+ *āva* + *vuñ* with the first long *ā* shortened by rule (2)]. Such forms are, however, rarely used.

The Passive of Causatives is formed regularly, in accordance with the rule already given; as, *tapāvavuñ*, 'to cause to warm;' Passive, *tapāvāvuñ*.

§ 15. *Irregular Causatives.*

Simple Stem.	*Caus. Stem.*
aḍ- (to impede) . . .	*aḍāḍ-*
bhaḷ- (to be mixed) . .	*bheḷav(a)-*
far- (to turn, *intr.*) . .	*ferav(a)-*
maḷ- (to meet, be got) .	*meḷav(a)-*
pī- (to drink)	*pā-*
ṭhar- (to be fixed) . .	*ṭharāv(a)-*, *ṭherav(a)-*
uchhar- (to grow up) .	*uchharāv(a)-*, *uchherāv(a)-*

§ 16. *The Compound Verb* (Sanyukta Kriyāpad).

Compound Verbs, that is verbs compounded of two simple verbs, play an important part in Gujarātī, as in most other Indian languages of the Sanskrit stock. They may be said to supply the place of verbs compounded with prepositions in Latin and Greek, or that of such particles as *on*, *down*, *away*, united to verbs in English. We may divide Compound Verbs into two classes:—(1) those properly so called, and (2) those less entitled to the appellation.

I.—*True Compounds.*

In these the two verbs are so united as to convey but

one idea. The signification of the second part of the compound is practically lost, but its use strengthens that of the first portion. The compound is formed by taking the *shortened form of the Connective Participle** of the first verb and attaching to it one of the following auxiliaries,—*nāñkhvuñ, devuñ, āpvuñ, javuñ, paḍvuñ, pāḍvuñ, śakvuñ, chukvuñ, rehevuñ, kāḍhvuñ, levuñ, āvavuñ, vaḷvuñ, vāḷvuñ,*—according to the sense required to be expressed. They may be tabulated in the following manner :—

1. *Potential.*—Formed by attaching *śakvuñ* to the shortened Connective Participle; as, *lakhvuñ*, 'to write,' Conn. Part., *lakhī-ne*; Compound, *lakhī śakvuñ*, 'to be able to write.' So also *jovuñ*, 'to see;' *joī śakvuñ*, 'to be able to see,' &c. E.g., *te nāno chhokro vāñchī śake chhe śuñ?* 'Can that little boy read?' *Śakvuñ* may be used in the *passive* when necessary; as, *Temthī pāchhuñ āvī śakāyuñ nahi*, 'they could not return.'

2. *Completive.*—Formed by adding *chukvuñ*, 'to finish,' to the same part of the principal verb; as, *khāvuñ*, 'to eat;' *khāī chukvuñ*, 'to finish eating;' *samjāvavuñ*, 'to cause to understand;' *samjāī chukvuñ*, 'to finish explaining.' E.g., *māro kutro te māñs khāī chukyo chhe*, 'my dog has finished eating that meat.'

3. *Intensitive.*—These are formed in the same way as the preceding, but the second part of the compound may

---

* As in Braj Bhāshā and Western Panjābī, *not* the *stem* of the verb as in Hindī.

be *devuñ, āpvuñ, nāñkhvuñ, kāḍhvuñ, vāḷvuñ, pāḍvuñ, levuñ,* as the meaning to be expressed may require. For example, *mārvuñ* is 'to strike,' but *mārī nāñkhvuñ* (Urdū مار ڈالنا) is 'to strike down,' *i.e.* 'to kill;' *pāvuñ,* 'to cause to drink;' *pāī devuñ,* 'to give to drink;' *mūkvuñ,* 'to put;' *mūkī nāñkhvuñ,* 'to put down at once,' 'throw down,' &c. When *devuñ* or *āpvuñ* are used in the second part of such compounds, the idea of *doing something for some one, doing a kindness to* some one, is generally implied. When *levuñ* is used, the sense of *taking for one's own advantage* is understood in English; as, *Te bādśāh Hindustān* JĪTĪ LEVĀNE *āvyo,* 'That king came to conquer (and take possession of) India.'

Similar compounds are formed with *intransitive* as well as *transitive* auxiliaries. For example, *Te rānī rogī thaī gaī chhe,* 'That queen has become ill;' *Tāro ghoḍo sagḷuñ pāṇī pī gayo,* 'Thy horse drank up all the water.' (The *idea* underlying such compounds will be best seen by translating idiomatically thus, 'That queen *has gone and got* ill;' 'thy horse *has gone and drunk* all the water.) The use of *āvavuñ* is somewhat similar; as, *Te chopḍī lakhāvī āvo,* 'having caused that book to be written, come.'

II.—*False Compounds.*

These are of various kinds, but the most important are those mentioned below. They cannot be regarded as true compounds, because the two verbs do not become one in meaning as in the examples given above.

1. *Frequentatives.*—Formed by affixing *karvuñ*, 'to make,' 'to do,' to the oblique form of the Past Participle,* as in Urdū. The latter remains unchanged throughout, while the auxiliary is conjugated in the usual manner. Example:—*bolyā karvuñ*, 'to be in the habit of speaking;' *māryā karvuñ*, 'to be in the habit of beating.' E.g., *Te mehetājī sadā chhokrāone bhaṇāvyā kare chhe*, 'That schoolmaster is always in the habit of teaching the boys.'

2. *Continuatives.*—Formed by adding to the Present Participle of any verb any part of the verbs *javuñ*, *āvavuñ*, or *rehevuñ*, as the case may be; as, *bolto* (m., *-i* f., *-uñ* n.) *rehevuñ*, 'to keep on talking;' *vāñchto* (*-i*, *-uñ*) *āvavuñ*, 'to come along reading:' as, *Ā sañsār jatõ rahe chhe*, 'this world is passing away;' *Te chālto jāy chhe*, 'he is going off.'

---

* In reality the form used is an indeclinable *gerund*, but for convenience the above method of describing it may be permitted.

CHAPTER VI.

Indeclinables (*Avyay*).

In Gujarātī, Adverbs, Postpositions, Conjunctions and Interjections do not admit of declension.

§ 1. I. *Adverbs* (Kriyāviśeshaṇ).

The adverb, as a general rule, precedes the word which it qualifies; as, *Te māṇas* ihāñ *rahe chhe*, 'that man dwells here.'

As in German, any adjective may become an adverb *in use*, i.e. may be used adverbially, but in such cases it *generally agrees with the subject of the verb in gender, number and case*, if it belongs to the class of Adjectives which admit (Cap. III., § 1) of declension. Example:—*Ā chhokro* sāro *vāñche chhe, paṇ tenī behen* sārī *vāñchtī nathī*, 'This boy reads *well*, but his sister does not read *well*.' Occasionally, however, the adjective in such sentences is put in the absolute singular neuter and is used as an ordinary adverb.

From the Pronouns *Ā, E, Je, Te, Ke*, Adverbs are formed denoting manner, place and time, in the following way:—

Ā, This.	*ām*, in this way.	*añhi*, here.	*āj*, to-day.
E, That.	*em*, thus.	*ahīñ*, *hyān*, here.	*atyāre*, then.
Je, Who.	*jem*, *jyam*, in which way.	*jyāñ*, where.	*jyāre*, when.
Te, That.	*tem*, *tyam*, thus.	*tyāñ*, there.	*tyāre*, then.
Ke, Who?	*kyam*, *kem*, how?	*kyāñ*, where?	*kyāre*, when?

Others formed from the same Pronouns are:—*Tāñhāñ*, *Tahīñ*, 'there;' *Kāñhāñ*, *Kahīñ*, 'where?' &c.

Such adverbs, and more especially those of *place* and *time*, are often governed by the postposition *-no*, m.; *-nī*, f.; *-nuñ*, n., and the compound thus formed is used as a declinable adjective; e.g., *Teo* tyāññā *lokomāñ maḷī gayā*, 'They mingled among the people (of there) of that place.' [Cf. *οἱ νῦν ἄνθρωποι, ὁ ἀεὶ βασιλεύς*, in Greek, and in English, 'The *then* King of France made a decree.']

§ 2. Adverbs, like Adjectives in Gujarātī, do not undergo any change to express the Comparative and Superlative degrees, but these are denoted in the same way as with adjectives.

'The more . . . the more' (Latin, *tanto . . . quanto; eo . . . quo*) is expressed by *Jem jem . . . tem tem;* as, Jem jem *nīche utartā jaīe*, tem tem *jhāḍī vadhāre āvatī jāy chhe*, 'The farther down one goes (we go), the more abundant does the brushwood become.'

The word *karīne*, Connective Participle of the verb *karvuñ*, 'to do,' is often used in an adverbial sense; as, *ghaṇuñ karīne*, 'often;' *teṇe karīne*, 'therefore;' *hāthe karīne,* 'manually,' 'by hand.' The following use of the word may conveniently be inserted here:—*Teno pahelo rājā Vikrām* karīne *thaī gayo,* 'Its first king *was called* Vikrām.' *Te deśne hamṇā Malabār* karīne *kahe chhe,* 'That country they now *name* Malabar.'

Foreign (chiefly Arabic and Persian) phrases are, in a corrupted form, introduced into Gujarātī, and there treated as simple adverbs; as, *belāśak* (بلا شكّ), 'doubtless;' *bīngunhe* (بي گناه ?), 'sinlessly.'

§ 3. I may be allowed in this place to notice a somewhat curious usage of the negative adverb *nahi.* It is well exemplified in the following sentence:—*Panjāb deśnā lokonā satyaguṇnī vāt temnā granthomāñthīj mālūm paḍe chhe,*—eṭluñj nahi, *paṇ bījā deśonā loko te deśnī śobhā jovā sāruñ āvatā hatā,*—'The report of the excellence of the people of the country of the Panjāb is known not from their own books (*lit.* falls known through their books, —*not so, but*), but [from the accounts of] people of other lands [who] used to come for the sake of seeing the beauty of that region.' Sentences similar to this in their use of the negative—asserting a thing for the purpose of strongly contradicting the assertion immediately after and thus *strengthening* the negative—are common.

The adverb *jyāre,* 'when,' is frequently and elegantly omitted (*vide* under Conjunctions); as, *te rājā marī gayo,* tyāre *tenā bhāīe rāj kīdhuñ,* '*When* that king died, then his brother reigned.'

§ 4. II. *Postpositions* (Nāmyogī).

Except the simple and genuine Postpositions, *-ne, -e, -thī, -thakī, -vatī, -no -nī -nuñ, -māñ,* all the rest were originally nouns in the locative case. In consequence of this they (1) possess *gender,* and (2) require the oblique case of *-no, -nī, -nuñ,* to interpose between them and the noun they govern. Frequently, however, this *possessive* postposition may be omitted, though when not expressed it is understood. E.g., *sāthe,* 'along with;' *te sipāī*-nī *sāthe,* 'along with that sepoy;' *ā rīti*-nī *pramāṇe,* or *ā rīti pramāṇe,* 'according to this method.'

The gender of some postpositions varies in different parts of Gujarāt.

The subjoined lists will show which of the Postpositions require *-nā* (m. and n. obl. of *-no*) before them, which *-nī* (f.), and which *-ne* (m. and n. locative of *-no*). If the same postposition occurs in more than one list, it will show that both usages are allowable.

Requiring *-nā.*

kartāñ	*sot*	*sudhī*	*vishe*	*lagaṇ*
vaḍe	*suddhāñ*	*sarkhuñ*	*vate*	*par*
vanā	*samet*	*maḷīne*	*vagar*	*upar*
vinā	*samīp*	*śivāy*	*lagī*	*haste*
sahit	*sambandhī*			

Requiring *-nī*.

agāu	*pāse*	*sāmuñ*	*mārafat*	*sāme*
agāḍī	*peṭhe*	*sāmāñ*	*māfak*	*sākshāt*
ārpār	*pachhī*	*sāthe*	*pramāṇe*	*sanmukh*
āgaḷ	*pār*	*hastak*	*heṭhe*	*chotaraf*
andar	*pūṭhaḷ*	*haste*	*heṭhaḷ*	*fartuñ*
āspās	*pūṭhe*	*bābat*	*nīche*	*vachmāñ*
kane	*pahelāñ*	*bahār*	*tale*	*mahīñ*
goḍe	*mele*	*bhaṇī*	*gam*	*māñhe*
joḍe	*vachche*	*barābar*	*mer*	*madhye*
pachhvāḍe	*vāñse*	*uparānt*	*taraf*	*vāñsaḷ*
pāchhaḷ	*sāmo* (adj.)	*sangāte*		

Requiring *-ne*.

kāje *māṭe* *līdhe* *vāste* *sāru(ñ)* *badle* *kāraṇe*

§ 5. Several postpositions are often affixed together to a noun, as in the following sentences:—(1) *Te ghar*māñthī *koī āvśe nahi*, 'From that house (*lit.* from in that house) no one will come;' *Ā deś*māññā *loko rogī chhe*, 'The people of (*of in*) that country are ill;' *E jhāḍ*parthī *mevo laī āvo*, 'Bring fruit from off (*lit.* 'from *on*') that tree.' Sometimes the long words thus formed look quite formidable, but they will be found easy to resolve into their component parts. *E.g.*, Paśchimbhaṇīnā *baḷvān deśomāñ temnī dolat-vishe bahu vāto chāltī*, 'Many stories were current in powerful *western* lands regarding their wealth.' The first word in this sentence is thus compounded, *Paśchim*, 'the west;' *bhaṇī*, 'direction,' 'towards,' and *nā*, pl. obl. of *no*, agreeing with *deśo*. It *might* have been even longer, *Paśchimnībhaṇīnā*. Sometimes such compounds of a noun and a postposition receive the adjectival [cap. viii., § 1, p. 92 (*o*)], termination *-lo*, *-lī*, *-luñ*; as, *Pachhī* Yūrop-khanḍmāñhelā *Yūnāndeśno Sikandar bādśāh śumāre savā be hajār varaspar Hindustān jītī levāne āvyo*, 'Formerly, two-and-a-quarter thousand years ago in number, Alexander, king of the land-of-Greece, which-is-in-the-continent-of-Europe—*lit.* king of the Europe-continent-within-(*adj. term.*) Greece-land—came to conquer India.'

In a sentence denoting *motion to a place*, there is no postposition required; as, *Te ghar gayo*, 'he went to the house.' If the noun denoting the place to which motion occurs ends in a consonant, in *-o* or in *-ī*, its form undergoes no alteration; but if it end in *-ā* or *-u*, these terminations are changed to *-e*; as, *Te loko Khaṇḍāḷe gayā chhe*, 'those people have gone to Khaṇḍāḷā.'

§ 6. *Use of the simple Postpositions.*

The simple or *proper* Postpositions, besides their general and obvious uses, which require no remark, are employed idiomatically in some instances, as will be seen from the examples given below.

(1) *-No* (*-nī*, *-nuñ*) often denotes the *material* of which a thing is composed; e.g., *Ā ghar lākḍā*nuñ *bandhāeluñ chhe*, 'this house is built *of* wood.'

It is also occasionally employed to denote the *time* of an

action; as, *Te rājā savārno jāge chhe,* 'that king awakens *in* the morning.' (Cf. Greek *νυκτός* and German Morgens.)

It is used as *of* in English in such phrases as *Sindhno mūlak,* 'the country *of* Sindh.'

Also in such constructions as, *Ā paṇḍit buddhino chālāk chhe,* 'This Paṇḍit is quick *of* comprehension.'

(2) *-Thī,* besides denoting *from* in all its meanings, also denotes *than* in comparison; as, *Te chhokro mārā bhāī*thī *moṭo thayo,* 'That boy grew bigger *than* my brother.' Also the instrument *with* which a thing is done; as, *bhālā*thī, '*with* a spear.' Also cause *through* which; as, *E bāiḍī dhūp*thī *rogī thaī gaī,* 'That woman became ill *through* the heat.' Also the agent after a *passive* verb; as, *Tenā*thī *e deś badho jītāyo nahi,* 'All that country was not conquered *by* him.' It also means *since*; as, *Traṇ varas*thī *te ā nagarmāñ vase chhe,* 'He has lived in this city for the last three years.' *-Thī* is also used with verbs of *fearing*; as, *Huñ rājā*thī *bīdho,* 'I feared the king.'

(3) *-Māñ,* besides meaning *in* and *into,* has also the sense of *on*; as, *Mugaṭ tenā māthā*māñ *hato,* 'The crown was *on* his head.' The difference (when there is any) between *-māñ* and *-e* in its locative sense is that the former means *in* or *into* and the latter *at,* though the latter has also the meaning of *in.* (In nouns of Class I., however [ch. ii., § 5, p. 32], this termination *never* has any but an *agential* meaning.)

(4) *-E.*—Except in the case mentioned above, this termination has two senses, (1) a *locative,* and (2) an *agential.*

In the former instance it is doubtless derived from the Sanskrit locative, in the latter from the Sanskrit *instrumental* case, which in nouns of the 1st Class *m.* terminates in *-ena* (e.g., *śivas,* nom., *śivena,* loc.). Hence some Gujarātī scholars write the postposition *-e* as *-eñ* in this agential significance.

When the termination *-e* is *locative,* or denotes anything but the *agential* relation, if the noun to which it is attached be preceded by a declinable adjective or a noun with the postposition *-no,* m. (or *-nuñ,* n.), *this is also put in the locative;* as, *Temne kabje,* 'in their grasp;' *bīje varase,* 'next year.'

But when the *-e* is *agential* this *does not* take place; as, *Prabhunā dūte mane kahyuñ,* 'The angel of the Lord said unto me;' *Bābarne tenā bāpe bhaṇāvyo hato,* 'His father had taught Bābar.'

This postposition *-e* has a large number of varieties of significance, some of which will be learnt from the following sentence*:—*Meñ māre hāthe tene māthe paghḍī bāndhī,* 'I with my own hand bound the *pagri* on his head.' It denotes *instrument, cause, measure of time, price, location,* &c. When it denotes *at* or *in* it may, like *māñ,* be followed by *-thī;* as, *te niśālethī nikaḷyo,* 'he came out of school.'

§ 7. III. *Conjunctions* (Vākyayogī *or* Ubhayānvayī).

These require little remark, though some few of them

* Quoted from Taylor's 'Gujarātī Bhāshāṇuñ Vyākaraṇ,' p. 37, § 79.

have peculiarities of use. For instance, *ke* and *athvā* both mean 'or,' but the former is used between nouns or single words, the latter between sentences; as, *Rājā* ke *rāṇī*, 'the king *or* the queen;' but *Te ā kām karśe*, athvā, *jo karī na śakśe, to marī jaśe*, 'He will do this work, *or*, if he cannot, then he will die.'

Instead of *ane*, 'and,' the shorter form *ne* is often used. This latter is distinguished from the postposition of the same form by the fact that the conjunction is not attached to the preceding word in writing and does not, of coursse require the oblique form of the word which precedes it.

If the former of two sentences connected with one another begins with *jo*, 'if,' expressed or understood (for it, like *jyāre*, 'when,' is often *understood*), the latter sentence must begin with *to*, 'then;' as, (*Jo*) *te āvśe*, *to huñ jaīś*, 'If he comes, then I shall go.' So also, if the former sentence contains such a word as *kadāpi*, *kadāchit* (*kadāch*), 'perhaps,' the latter must begin with *to*, *tathāpi* or *topaṇ*, 'then,' 'yet.'

Ke, 'that,' is used in quoting the words of a speaker, and is followed by the *oratio recta*.

§ 8. IV. *Interjections* (Kevaḷprayogī).

These require no special remark, being used in Gujarātı much as such words are in other languages. A few of the most common are:—*O*, *e*, *re*, *are*, *ere*, *oy*, *alī*, *alyā*, *vāh*, *vhāvā*, *chhī*, *āh*, *hā*, *hāhā*, *he*, &c.

CHAPTER VII.

Numerals.

The numerical signs in Gujarātī are: ૧, ૨, ૩, ૪, ૫, ૬, ૭, ૮, ૯, ૧૦, = 1, 2, 3, &c. Fractions are written thus:—$\frac{1}{4}$ = ૦। ; $\frac{1}{2}$ = ૦।। ; $\frac{3}{4}$ = ૦।।। ; as $1\frac{1}{2}$ = ૧।। ; $3\frac{3}{4}$ = ૩।।।.

§ 1. The Cardinals are :—

1. *ek*
2. *be*
3. *traṇ*
4. *chār*
5. *pānch*
6. *chha*
7. *sāt*
8. *āṭh*
9. *nav*
10. *das, daś*
11. *agiār*
12. *bār*
13. *ter*
14. *chaud*
15. *pandar*
16. *soḷ, sol*
17. *satar, sattar*
18. *arāḍh, aḍhār*
19. *ogaṇīs*
20. *vīs*
21. *ekvīs*
22. *bāvīs*
23. *trevīs*
24. *chovīs*
25. *pachīs*
26. *chhavīs*
27. *sattāvīs*
28. *aṭh(ṭh)āvīs*
29. *ogaṇvīs*
30. *trīś, trīs*
31. *ektrīs*
32. *batrīs*
33. *tetrīs*
34. *chotrīs*
35. *pāntrīs*
36. *chhatrīs*
37. *sāḍtrīs*
38. *āḍtrīs*
39. *ogaṇchāḷīs*
40. *chāḷīs*
41. *ektāḷīs*
42. *betāḷīs*
43. *t(r)etāḷīs*
44. *chuñvāḷīs* (*chuñmāḷīs*)
45. *pistāḷīs*
46. *chhetāḷīs*
47. *suḍtāḷīs* (*saḍtāḷīs*)
48. *aḍtāḷīs*
49. *ogaṇparhās*

50. *pachās*
51. *ekāvan*
52. *bāvan*
53. *trepan*
54. *chopan*
55. *panchāvan*
56. *chappan*
57. *sattāvan*
58. *aṭhṭhāvan*
59. *ogaṇsāṭh*
60. *sāṭh*
61. *eksaṭh*, *ekseṭh*
62. *bāsaṭh*, *-seṭh*, (&c.)
63. *tresaṭh*
64. *chosaṭh*
65. *pānsaṭh*
66. *chhāsaṭh*
67. *saḍsaṭh*
68. *aḍsaṭh*
69. *aganoter* (*agaṇoter*)
70. *siter*
71. *ikoter*
72. *bhoter* (*bohoter*)
73. *toter* (*tohoter*)
74. *chuñmoter*
75. *panchoter*
76. *chhoter*
77. *sattoter* (*sittoter*)
78. *aṭhṭhoter* (*iṭhṭhoter*)
79. *agnoeñśī* (*ogaṇyāsī*)
80. *eñśī*, *heñsī*
81. *ekāśī*, *-āsī*, (&c.)
82. *bāśī*
83. *trāśī*, *tyāsī*
84. *chorāśī*
85. *panchāśī*
86. *chhāśī*
87. *sattāśī*
88. *aṭhṭhāśī*
89. *nevāśī* (*nevyāsī*)
90. *nevuñ*
91. *ekāṇuñ*
92. *bāṇuñ*
93. *trāṇuñ*
94. *chorāṇuñ*
95. *panchāṇuñ*
96. *chhannuñ*
97. *sattāṇuñ*
98. *aṭhṭhāṇuñ*
99. *navāṇuñ* (*navyāṇuñ*)
100. *soñ*, *so*
200. *baseñ*
300. *traṇseñ*
400. *chārseñ*
500. *pānchseñ*
1,000. *ek hajār*
2,000. *be hajār*
100,000. *lākh*
1,000,000. *das lākh*
10,000,000. *karoḍ*

It will be noticed that in some instances more than one form is used.

§ 2. *Ordinals.*—These are: 1st, *pehelo, -ī, -uñ*; 2nd, *bījo*; 3rd, *trījo*; 4th, *chotho*; 5th, *pāncho*; 6th, *chhaṭho*; 7th, *sātmo*; 8th, *āṭhmo*; the ordinals after the 6th being formed by attaching the ending *-mo, -mī, -muñ*, to the cardinals. The ordinals are regular declinable adjectives.

Multiplicatives.—The formation of these will be clear from the following examples:—*bamaṇuñ*, 'double;' *tramaṇuñ*, 'treble;' *chogaṇuñ*, 'fourfold;' *chhagaṇuñ*, 'six-fold.' These (the forms I have given being *neut.*), are declined regularly; as, *dasgaṇ-o, -ī, -uñ*, 'ten-fold,' &c. Another series is formed by adding *-vaḍuñ* to the cardinal; as, *bevaḍo, -ī, -uñ*, 'double;' *trevaḍo, -ī, -uñ*, 'triple,' &c.

Fractions.—One quarter, *pā*; one half, *aḍḍho* or *ardho*; three quarters, *poṇo*; one and a quarter, *savā*; one and a half, *doḍh* or *dohoḍ*; one and three quarters, *poṇā be*; two and a quarter, *savā be*; two and a half, *aḍhī* or *haḍī*; three and a quarter, *savā traṇ*; three and a half, *sāḍā traṇ*; four and a half, *sāḍā chār*, &c. So also 75 may be expressed by *poṇo so* (*i.e.* $\frac{3}{4}$ of 100); 250 by *aḍhīseñ* ($2\frac{1}{2}$ hundreds), &c.

The addition of *-e* to a numeral denotes 'all'; as, *traṇ*, 'three; *traṇe*, 'all three.' 'Both' is denoted by *beu*, and also by *bandhe* and *banne*. *Eke* means 'just one.'

'And' between numerals which form part of one number is omitted in Gujarātī; as, *ek soñ traṇ*, 'one hundred *and* three.'

§ 3. The following are a few *nouns* denoting number:—

Beluñ, 'a couple.'
ṭako, 'a triad.'
chok, a number containing four.
panchak, " " five.
chhak, " " six.
sātuñ, " " seven.
āṭhuñ, " " eight.
navak, " " nine.
dasak, " " ten.
koṭī, } a score.
kuṇṭī, }
sainkuñ, } one hundred.
sekḍuñ, }

CHAPTER VIII.

FORMATION OF WORDS: COMPOUNDS.

§ 1. The great majority of words in the Gujarātī language are derived from the Sanskrit. It would be out of place here to explain the formation of Sanskrit compounds,—information which the student may easily obtain, if he pleases, from Monier Williams' "Sanskrit Grammar," ch. viii., sect. 1. But some words are in Gujarātī formed by certain Gujarātī affixes, the principal of which necessarily find a place here.

(*a*) To denote 'state,' *-paṇ* or *-paṇuñ* is added to adjectives or nouns; as, *sagpaṇ*, 'relationship;' *bāḷpaṇ*, 'childhood;' *uparīpaṇuñ* (from *uparī*, 'overseer'), 'superintendence;' *nādānpaṇuñ*, 'ignorance.'

(*b*) To the stems of some verbs and adjectives *-āī* is added; as, *murkhāī*, 'folly;' *chaturāī*, 'cleverness,' 'cuteness.'

(*c*) The termination *-ī* has many meanings, as will be seen from the following examples:—*rogī*, 'sick' (from *rog*, 'disease'); *ghaḍīāḷī*, 'a watchmaker' (from *ghaḍīāḷ*, 'a watch, clock'); Hindustānī, 'a native of Hindūstān.'

(*d*) The affix *-īyo*, *īo*, *yo*, *aiyo*, forms adjectives and nouns; as, *bhūkhyo*, 'hungry' (from *bhūkh*); *bhomīo*, 'a guide;' *gavaiyo*, 'a singer.'

(*e*) *Āṭ*, *-āṭo*, *-vaṭ*, *-vaṭo*; as, *gamrāṭ*, 'confusion;' *jhapāṭo*, 'a blast;' *sāchvaṭ*, 'truthfulness;' *bhogvaṭo*, 'sensual pleasure.'

(*f*) *-Vān*, *-vant*, denote 'possessing;' as, *baḷvān*, 'strong;' *dhanvant*, 'wealthy.'

(*g*) The addition of *-ḍo*, *-ḍī*, *-ḍuñ*, forms substantives and adjectives, originally (and still in many cases) *diminutives*; as, *nāv*, 'a ship' (*n.* in Gujarātī, though *f.* in Sanskṛit, Latin and Greek); *nāvḍī*, 'a boat;' *nāvduñ*, 'a large vessel:' *loḍhuñ*, 'iron;' *loḍhī*, 'an iron bread-pan:' *gāmḍuñ*, 'a small village.'

(*h*) *-Tā*, *-tva*, form abstract nouns; as, *pavitratā*, 'holiness;' *dāstva*, 'slavery.'

(*i*) *-Vāḷ* denotes 'keeper;' *koṭvāḷ*, 'commander of a fort,' 'police-officer.'

(*j*) *-Vāḷo*, *-vāḷī*, *-vāḷuñ*, forms nouns and adjectives; as, *vichārvāḷo*, 'thoughtful;' *ṭopīvāḷo*, 'hat-wearer (European); &c. This affix is often added to the latter of two words closely united together in a sentence; as, *sonerī sājvāḷā hāthīo*, 'elephants with golden trappings;' *māṭhā pariṇāmvāḷī rūḍhīo*, 'corrupt idioms.'

(*k*) The usual termination added to the verbal stem to denote the 'agent' is *-nār*; as, *bechnār*, 'a seller.'

(*l*) Another (Sanskṛit) is *ak*; as, *pāḷak*, 'supporter' (from *pāḷvuñ*, 'to nourish, rear'); *geṭāpāḷak*, 'shepherd.'

(*m*) The Persian affix *-dār* ('possessor') is sometimes

added to Gujarātī words; as, *vahīvaṭdār*, 'officer,' 'collector' (from *vahīvaṭ*).

(n) *-āḷ*, *-āḷo* (*-ī*, *-uñ*), forms adjectives; as, *rasāḷ*, 'juicy,' 'sappy,' 'fertile' (from *ras*, 'juice'); *retāḷ*, 'sandy,' for *ret*, 'sand;' *muchhāḷo*, 'a man with a long mustachio' (from *muchh*, 'mustache'). So also, *Sundar pīchhāḷāñ pakshī*, 'beautifully feathered birds.'

(o) *-ḷu* is used somewhat similarly; as, *dayāḷu*, 'merciful' (from *dayā*, 'mercy'). *-Lo*, *-lī*, *-luñ*, is another termination to form adjectives; as, *Sindhmāñhelā loko*, 'people in Sindh.'

(p) *-at* and *-atī* added to the root of verbs form nouns; as *gamat*, 'amusement' (from *gamvuñ*, 'to approve of'); *gaṇatī*, 'numbering' (from *gaṇvuñ*, 'to count').

(q) *-nā* forms a few nouns; as, *sūchnā*, 'a suggestion' (from *sūchavavuñ*, 'to suggest').

(r) *ādi* is added with the meaning of *etc.*; as, *Krishṇ, Devī, Śivādi*, 'Kṛishna, Devī, Śiva, &c.'

§ 2. Feminine nouns are often formed from masculines, denoting living beings, by the change of the masculine termination or the addition of one peculiarly feminine.

(a) If the masc. noun ends in *-o*, the fem. takes *-ī*; as, *chhokro*, 'a boy,' *chhokrī*, 'a girl;' *ghoḍo*, 'a horse,' *ghoḍī*, 'a mare;' *beṭo*, 'a son,' *beṭī*, 'a daughter.' Also *dev*, 'a god,' *devī*, 'a goddess.'

(b) When the masc. ends in *ī* or a consonant, the termination fem. is *-aṇ*, *-eṇ*, *-aṇī* or *-āṇī*; as, *mochī*, 'a bootmaker,' *mochaṇ*, 'a bootmaker's wife;' *bhāī*, 'a brother,' *beheṇ*, 'a sister' (irreg.); *śeṭh*, 'a merchant, &c., *śeṭhāṇī*, 'a merchant's wife;' *paṭel*, 'headman of a village,' *paṭelāṇī*, 'a Paṭel's wife;' *piśāch*, 'a goblin,' *piśāchaṇī*, 'a female goblin.'

Another fem. termination is *-ḍī*; as, *chākar*, 'a man-servant,' *chākarḍī*, 'a female servant;' *ūndar*, 'a rat,' *ūndarḍī*, 'a female rat;' *Bhīl*, 'a Bhīl,' *Bhīlḍī*, 'a female Bhīl;' *gulām*, 'a slave,' *gulāmḍī*, 'a female slave' (contemptuously).

(c) Somewhat irregular are:—*nar*, 'male,' *nārī*, 'a female;' *rājā*, 'a king,' *rāṇī*, 'a queen;' *brāhmaṇ*, 'a Brahmaṇ,' *brāhmaṇī*, 'a female Brahmaṇ;' *vāṇīo*, 'a shopkeeper, *vāṇīeṇ*, 'a shopkeeper's wife.'

§ 3. *Compounds.*

Gujarātī compounds (as distinguished from Sanskrit compound words introduced into the language) are generally formed by the mere juxtaposition of the simple words. They will be best illustrated by a few examples. E.g :—

Rājdarbār, 'a royal court,' 'a levee;' fr. *rāj* or *rājā* and *darbār*.

Gharkām, 'housework;' fr. *ghar*, 'house,' and *kām*, 'work.'

Rītbhāt, 'manners and customs.'

Kav'tārūp, 'poetical.'

Yūropkhaṇḍ, 'the continent of Europe.'

Vāyubharelī mashak, 'an air-filled water-skin.'

Hīrāmāṇeke jaḍelāñ tathā motīnāñ ghareṇāñ pahere chhe, 'They wear ornaments set with diamonds-and-rubies and made of pearls.' Here the first word is composed of *hīrā*, pl. of *hīro*, 'a diamond;' *māṇek*, 'a ruby,' and the postposition *-e*.

A slightly different kind of compound is formed by inserting *o* between two repetitions of the same word; as, *deśodeś*, 'from country to country;' *hajārohajār*, 'thousands of thousands.'

Not a few nouns and verbs are formed by adding an unmeaning word to one which has the meaning to be expressed; as, *farvuñ*, 'to turn;' *farvuñ harvuñ*, 'to walk about.' (Cf. Panjābī, *pāṇī-wāṇī*, *roṭī-woṭī*; Urdū, *shor-bhor*; Persian, *āb-māb*; French, *pêle-mêle*; English, *shilly-shally*.)

CHAPTER IX.

Syntax.

Much of the Syntax of the language has already been introduced where it seemed likely to be most easily remembered. In this chapter we deal with the few points which still remain to be elucidated, but omit a detailed account of those common to most Indo-European tongues, regarding which error is almost impossible.

§ 1. In Gujarātī, the usual order of words in a sentence is,—(1) Subject; (2) Indirect Object; (3) Direct Object; (4) Predicate: but this may be altered for the sake of emphasis.

When a number of nouns, all in the same case and governed by one and the same postposition, occur in a sentence, the postposition is generally attached only to the last noun, though they are all in the oblique form. As, *Te rājāe bahu loko, purusho, strīo ne chhokrāñone mārī nāñkhyāñ*, 'That king killed many people—men, women and children.'

But in such sentences it is a common practice to put the whole of the nouns in the *absolute* state, and then place the *oblique* plural of the pronoun *e* or *te* after them, adding the postposition required to the pronoun only. As, *Mārā pitā, mārā mitro ne mārā dīkrāo*, teoe *ā kām kīdhuñ*; 'My father, my friends and my sons, *they* did this work.'

If two or more nouns of the same gender have a common predicate, that predicate is plural, but agrees with the subjects in gender. But if the subjects be of different genders, the predicate is put in the *neuter* * plural. As, (1) *Māro dīkro ane teno mitr* sārā *chhe*, 'My son and his friend are good.' But (2) *Māro dīkro ne mārī dīkrī* sārāñ *chhe*, 'My son and my daughter are good.' *Sulochanī ne teno bhāī nagarbhaṇī* hiṇdyāñ, 'Sulochanī and her brother walked towards the city.'

§ 2. The predicate, whether it be a verb or an adjective, may be put in the *plural* to show respect, even if the subject be in the *singular*. In such cases, if the subject be *masculine* the predicate is also masculine; but if the subject be *feminine*, respect requires that the predicate be NEUTER plural. As, (1) *Rājā* āvyā *chhe*, 'the king has come;' but, (2) *temnī sāthe rāṇī paṇ* āvyāñ *chhe*, 'with him the queen has also come.'

If there be in a sentence several subjects of different genders joined by the *disjunctive* conjunctions *vā*, *āthvā*, *ke*, the predicate agrees in gender and number with that nearest to it; as, *teno ghoḍo* ke *tenī gāy marī gaī*, 'his horse *or* his cow died.'

When an impersonal verb is put in the passive, the noun which was the subject of the verb is put in the oblique

* This strange idiom occurs also in the Icelandic language.

form with -*thī*, and the verb becomes impersonal neuter; as, *Huñ beṭho*, 'I sat,' which becomes *mārāthī besāyuñ*.

§ 3. The Infinitive and Gerundive when used as subjects require the agent, if a noun, to be put in the oblique form with -*e*; and if a pronoun, in what we may call the dative (*māre, tamāre*, &c.); as, *Strīoe ā chopḍī vāñchvī chhe*, 'Women ought to read this book;' *māre e kām karvuñ nathī*, 'I must not do that.' If the Infinitive when used as a subject governs any object, then it must agree with its object in gender and number, though not in case; as, *Māṇase amne Devnā marmonā kārbhārīonā jevā* gaṇvā, 'Men should account us as stewards of the mysteries of God.' In such sentences the verb *to be* is often omitted.

The infinitive may be declined exactly as a noun, and the gerundive as an adjective. The *oblique singular* of the infinitive, with or without -*ne*, is used after another verb to denote purpose, &c.; as, *tene hiāñ rehevā dyo*, 'let him stay here;' *te bādśāh deś jītī levā(ne) āvyo*, 'that king came to conquer the country.'

§ 4. The preterite of a verb, both active and passive, may be used as a gerund by affixing any postposition and changing the absolute form of the verb into the oblique; as, *te jaṇāyo*, 'he was born;' *te jaṇāyā vagar*, 'after he was born;' *Parameśvarnī stuti kīdhā pachhī*, 'after having praised God;' *maraṇ pāmyā pehelāñ*, 'before having died;' *paisā līdhā vinā*, 'without having taken the money.' A very slightly altered construction is seen in *Sikandarnā muā pachhī*, 'after Alexander's having died.'

The 1st Plural Aorist is used quite indefinitely in many cases; as, *Nīche* āvīe, *tyāre medānmāñ ek moṭuñ koṭ dekh-āśe*, 'When *we* (*i.e.* one comes) come down, then a large fort will be seen in the plain.' 'We' is sometimes used in English in this sense, but we more commonly say 'you' or 'one.'

§ 5. The Gujarātī language can express several varieties of meaning in the Imperative:—

(1) The simple Imperative is used when it is desired that the command be immediately executed; as, *tame ā chopḍī vāñcho*, 'Read this book.'

(2) If the command is intended to be obeyed after some interval, the *j* forms of the Future are employed; as, *tame ā chopḍī vāñchjo*, 'you will read this book.'

(3) If a polite injunction is intended, the ordinary Future is employed; as, *tame ā chopḍī vāñchśo*, 'you will (kindly) read this book.'

(4) To imply *duty*, the Gerundive is employed; as, *tamāre ā chopḍī* vāñchvī, 'You *should* read this book.'

§ 6. The negative of the simple imperative is formed by adding *mā* or *māñ* after it; as, *tame ā chopḍī vāñcho mā*, 'Don't read this book.'

That of the second form above given—the Future Imperative—is formed by placing the verb in the *present participle* and adding *nahi*; as, *tame ā chopḍī vāñchtā nahi*, 'You *shall not* read this book.'

The verb *devuñ* is used with the *oblique* infinitive of

another verb to imply *permission* (as *denā* is in Hindī and Urdū); as, *Tane e kām karvā huñ daīś nahi*, 'I shall not permit thee to do that work.'

§ 7. *Idiomatic Phrases.*

In Gujarātī the 1st Personal Pronoun *precedes* the second, and the second the third, as in Latin. Thus instead of saying 'He and I,' we say in Gujarātī, 'I and he' (*huñ ne te*).

Instead of saying, 'Neither my friend nor his daughter has gone,' we more commonly say, 'My friend or his daughter, no one has gone,' (*māro mitr ke tenī dikrī, koī gayuñ nathī*), the *koī* taking a *neuter* participle because it refers to either of two subjects, one of which is masculine and the other feminine. In similar sentences, when *things* are mentioned instead of persons, *kaīñ* is used instead of *koī*.

As the *oratio obliqua* is unknown in Gujarātī, the *oratio recta* is used instead. Such a sentence therefore as, 'The queen said that she would go home,' would be rendered thus, *Rāṇīe kahyuñ ke, huñ ghėr jaīś*, (literally, "The queen said that, 'I shall go home'").

When the subject in a sentence is a subordinate sentence, as, 'I heard that he had gone,' it is often better to put the subordinate sentence first, and then to place *e* or *te* after it; as, *Te gayo hato, e meñ sāmbhaḷyuñ* (literally, 'He had gone,—this I heard').

A *title* in Gujarātī, as in most Sanskritic languages

follows the proper name to which it is attached; as, *Rāmdās Śeṭh,* almost = 'Mr. Rāmdās.'

In interrogative sentences no change in the order of the words occurs, but *śuñ,* 'what?' is placed either before or after the sentence; as, *Śuñ te āvyo chhe?* 'What? has he come?'—or, *te āvyo chhe śuñ?* Frequently *ke* takes the place of *śuñ* at the end of such a sentence, and sometimes *both* are used together; as, *teo chālī gayā chhe ke śuñ?* 'Have they gone away?' (literally, 'Have they gone away, or what?')

APPENDIX A.

There are many words in Gujarātī which occur in other languages also in a more or less varied form. Some of these are pure Gujarātī words derived from the Sanskrit; others are taken from Arabic, Persian, &c. A few observations upon the forms which words of both classes assume in Gujarātī may perhaps be found useful, especially to those acquainted with any of the languages above mentioned.

While Hindī shows a preference for the sound *b*, Gujarātī prefers *v*. Hence in many instances a vocable beginning with *b* in Hindī has *v* as its first letter in Gujarātī. E.g., Hin. *banniā*, Guj. *vāṇīo*: Hin. *bikhai*, Guj. *viśe*: Hin. *binā*, Guj. *vinā*: Hin. *parbbat*, Guj. *parvat*, &c. Here Gujarātī resembles the Sanskrit more closely than spoken Hindī.

Gujarātī also prefers *ā* to *a*: hence *mākhan* for Hin. *makkhan*: Guj. *mākhī* for Hin. *makkhī*.

But *ai* becomes *e*, *au* becomes *o* in Gujarātī; as, Guj. *pēdā* for Urdu and Pers. پَیدا : *besvuñ* for Hin. *baiṭhnā* : *pesvuñ* for Hin. *paiṭhnā*: Guj. *ōlād* for Arab. اَولاد : Guj. *mot* for Arab. مَوت : Guj. *tōbā* for Arab. تَوبَہ : Guj. *londī* for Hin. *laundī*.

And *e* in Hin. sometimes becomes *ā* in Guj.; as, Hin. *mera*, Guj. *māro*: Hin. *terā*, Guj. *tāro*.

U is usually unchanged, but sometimes becomes *a*; as, Hin. *tum*, Guj. *tame*: Hin. *tumhārā*, Guj. *tamāro*.

Hindī *ṛ* becomes *ḍ*, and *ṛh* becomes *ḍh* in Guj.; as, *doḍvuñ* for *dauṛnā*; *chaḍhvuñ* for *chaṛhnā*.

Hindī *ṭh* sometimes becomes *s*; as, Hin. *paiṭhnā*, Guj. *pesvuñ*.

Such words as have *i* in the stem in Hindī have generally *a* instead in Gujarātī; as, Hin. *bigaṛnā*, Guj. *vagaḍvuñ*: Hin. *likhnā*, Guj. *lakhvuñ*: Hin. *milnā*, Guj. *maḷvuñ*. But *i* in Arabic and Persian words is generally represented by *e* (pronounced somewhat *short*) in Guj.; as, Guj. *sāheb* for Arab. صاحِب: Guj. *hākem* for Arab. حاكِم.

A before *h* in Arabic words is changed into *e* in Gujarātī; as, Guj. *sehelo* for Arab. سَهل: Guj. *vehem* (and contracted *vem*) for Arab. وَهْم. Similarly, Pers. شَهْر becomes in Guj. *śeher* and *śaher*: Arab. and Pers. مَحْنَت becomes Guj. *mehnat*: Arab. رَحْم becomes Guj. *rehem*.

Sanskrit *vy* (Hindī *by*), followed by a vowel, often becomes *ve*; as, Guj. *vehevār* = Hin. *vyavahār*: Guj. *vepār* for Hin. *byupār*.

Arabic ق (*q*) becomes *kh* if it occurs after a vowel;

as, Guj. *vakhat*, Arab. وَقْت. Otherwise it is generally changed into *k*; as, Guj. *kabūl*, Arab. قبُول.

The *z* sounds of Urdū and Persian (and of the letters ذ ض ظ in words introduced from Arabic into those languages) become *j* in Gujarātī; as, *jūlam* for ظلُم: *jakāt* for زکاة.

The double letters in such words as حَقّ, مُحَمَّد, مُدَّت, &c., when introduced into Gujarātī, become single; as, *hak*, *Mahamad*, *mudat* (or *mudad*).

Sometimes letters are transposed; as, Guj. *gunhā* for Pers. گُناه: Guj. *ṭīpvuñ* for Hin. *pīṭnā*.

Gujarātī has a preference for the sounds of *ḷ* and *ṇ* after long vowels, in this resembling Panjābī rather than Hindī. *Ḍ* sometimes takes the place of the Panjābī *ḷ*; as, Panj. *uṭhāḷnā*, Guj. *uṭhāḍvuñ*.

Sometimes an extra long vowel *ā* is inserted in Gujarātī in words borrowed from Persian; as, Guj. *śāhājādo* and *śāhjādo* for Pers. شاهزاده: Guj. *bāhādurī* for Pers. بَهادُري.

The Arabic letters ع and ح when they occur at the end of a word without a long vowel prefixed become *ā* and *e* respectively in Gujarātī; as, جَمْع, Guj. *jamā*: فَتْح, Guj. *fate*.

W in Hin. sometimes becomes *m* in Guj.; as, Hin. *pāñchwāñ*, Guj. *pāñchmo*: West Panjābī *pāwaṇā*, Guj. *pāmvuñ*.

In adverbial terminations, the Urdū *yūñ* (Old Hin. *yoñ*) becomes *-em* in Guj.; as, Old Hin. *tyoñ*, Hin. and Urdu *tyūñ*, Guj. *tem*.

In Gujarātī, *ū* and *ī* are frequently substituted for *u* and *i*, and *vice versa*.

If a word taken from another language *ends* in *-ā* or *-a*, this generally becomes *-o* in Guj., but occasionally changes to *-uñ*; as, Guj. *mevo*, from Pers. مَیوه : Guj. *śāhājādo* for Pers. شاهزاده : but Guj. *paranduñ* for Pers. پرَندَه.

Many words are formed by reduplicating the stem; as, *mārāmārī*, 'quarrel,' from *mārvuñ*, 'to strike.'

APPENDIX B.

TRANSLITERATION.

In order to give the student practice in transliteration before proceeding to the Second Part, we here append a few lines of Gujarātī with a transliteration in accordance with the system adopted in this Grammar.

સારો પવન જોઈને પછી અમે બોર્નિઓ બેટમાંથી
Sāro pavan joīne pachhī ame Bornio beṭmāñthi

નીકળ્યા, પણ આગળ ચાલતાં તોફાન લાગવા માડ્યું.
nīkaḷyā, paṇ āgaḷ chāltāñ tofān lāgvā māḍyuñ.

કેટલાક દહાડા લગી તો અમારૂં વહાણ ઊછળતુંજ
Keṭlāk dahāḍā lagī to amāruñ vahāṇ ūchhaḷtuñj

રહ્યું. છેવટે પવન નરમ પડ્યો, અને દરિયો જરા
rahyuñ. Chheraṭe pavan narm paḍyo, ane dariyo jarā

ધીમો થયો, એટલે બહુ છેટે અમે એક મછવો ડબકાં
dhīmo thayo, eṭle bahu chheṭe ame ek machhvo ḍabakāñ

ખાતો દીઠો. દૂરબીનમાંથી જોયું તો કેટલાંક આદમી
khāto dīṭho. Dūrbīnmāñthī joyuñ to keṭlāñk ādmī

મારા બાપે દીઠાં, અને તે દુઃખની નિશાનીનો વાવટો
mārā bāpe dīṭhāñ, ane te duhkhnī niśānīno vāvaṭo

ચઢાવતાં હોય એવાં જણાયાં. તેથી અમે અમારૂં
chaḍhāvatañ hoy evāñ jaṇāyāñ. Tethī ame amāruñ

વહાણ તેણીતરફ લેઈ ગયા, પણ દરિયાની ભારે
vahāṇ teṇītaraf leī gayā, paṇ dariyānī bhāre

છોળોને લીધે ત્યાં પહોંચીને તે મછવામાંહેના
chhoḷone līdhe tyāñ pahoñchīne te machhvāmāñhenā

લોકને અમારા ઝાઝપર લેતાં ઘણી વાર લાગી.
lokne amārā jhājhpar letāñ ghaṇī vār lāgī.

તેપર પાંચ આદમી હતાં, તેમાં માત્ર એક જણનેજ
Tepar pāñch ādmī hatāñ, temāñ mātr ek jaṇnej

બોલવાની શુદ્ધિ હતી.
bolvānī śuddhi hatī.

"Finding the wind favourable, we then left the island of Borneo, but as we went forward a storm began to come on. For some days accordingly our vessel continued to toss about. At last the wind fell ('fell quiet'), and the sea became somewhat calm; then very far off we saw a boat rolling. When looked at through the telescope, my father saw (in it) several persons, and they were perceived to be flying the distress signal-flags. Therefore we brought our vessel towards them, but on account of the heavy sea-billows much time was spent in arriving there and taking the people in the boat on board our own ship. There were five persons on board it, and among them only one had sufficient consciousness to speak."

PART II.

GUJARATI READING LESSONS.

INDEX.

GUJARĀTĪ READING LESSONS.

I. MUHAMMAD.

કોરેશ નામની અરબ લોકોમાં એક ઉંચી જાત છે, તેના સ્થાપનારાના વંશમાં મહમદ જન્મ્યો હતો. તે હાશિમના કુળનો હતો, અને તેના વંશોનાં નામ અરબી વંશાવળીઓમાં ચોકસાઈથી રાખેલાં છે. હાશેમનો છોકરો અબ્દુલ્ મોતાલેબ્ એકસો દશ વર્ષની ઉમર સુધી જીવ્યો. અબ્દુલ્લા નામનો તેનો એક નાહાનો છોકરો વાહેબની ખુબસુરત છોકરી આમિના સાથે પરણ્યો. આ બે જણને ઘરે મહમદ ઈસવી સન* ૫૭૦ ના વર્ષમાં મક્કા શેહેરમાં જન્મ્યો. તેના જન્મ્યા પેહેલાં અથવા તેના બચપણામાં તેનો બાપ મરી ગયો; અને તેની મા પણ તેને આઠ વર્ષનો મેહેલીને મરી ગઈ. તેને વારસામાં માત્ર પાંચ ઉંટ, અને એક ગુલામડી એટલું આપ્યું, તેથી તેને તેના દાદાના હાથ તળે રેહેવું પડયું. મહમદને

* The contraction for this is ઈ. સ.

તેના દાદાએ મરતી વેળાએ તેના છોકરા અબુ-તાલેબ, જેને તેની માલમતા મળી, તેને સ્વાધીન કર્યો. મહમદ બરોબર વચનો થયો* તારે તેણે તેને વેપારનું કામ સીખવ્યું. તે પચીસ વર્ષનો થયો તાંહાં સુધી પોતાના કાકાની ચાકરીમાં રહ્યો; એટલીજ વાત તેના બચપણા વિશેની માલુમ છે.

મૂસા તથા ઈશુ ઈશ્વરના પ્રાચીન મોકલેલાઓ, અને મહમદના પૂર્વાધિકારીઓ, જારે જન્મ્યા તારે જેવા ચમત્કારો થયા હતા તેવાજ ચમત્કારો મહમદ જન્મ્યો તારે પણ થયા, એવું મુસલમાની કિતાબોના લખનારાઓ લખેછે. તેઓ લખેછે કે મહમદ પેગંમબર જન્મ્યો તે વેળાએ એક પ્રકાશ એવો તો થયો હતો કે તેથી સિરીઆ દેશના સઘળા કીલ્લાઓ, શેહેરો, અને ગામડાંઓમાં તેથી ઉજાસ પડ્યો હતો; તથા સાવા સરોવરનાં પાણી બિલકુલ સુકાઈ ગયાં હતાં, તેથી તેઉપર એક શેહેર બંધાયું હતું; તથા એક ધરતીકંપ થયો હતો, તેથી ઈરાનના રાજાના મોહોલના ચઉદ મનારા પડી ગયા હતા; તથા પારસી લોકોનો પવિત્ર આતશ હોલવાઈ ગયો હતો;

* In this sentence supply *jāre* (*jyāre*) because of the *tāre* following (Gr. Cap. VI. § 3, fin.). Examples of this continually occur.

અને ચંદ્ર તથા તારા ઉપર વસનારા અશુદ્ધ આત્માઓ કાહાડી મુકાયા હતા, અને તેઓથી પૃથ્વી ઉપર મુર્તીઓઆં પાછું આવી શકાયું નહીં, અને દેવવાણી થઈ શકી નહીં. તે કિતાબોના લખનારાઓ એથી પણ વધારે એવું લખેછે કે તે બાળકે, આ દુનીઆમાં જનમ ધરતાંજ, ઘુટણીએ પડીને પોતાના હાથ આકાશની તરફ ઉંચા કર્યા હતા, અને એવી રીતે આ શબ્દો બોલ્યો હતો, "ઈશ્વર મોટો છે; ઈશ્વર એકજ છે; અને હું તેનો પેગંમબર છું." મહમદના જનમ વિશે આ અને એવીજ બીજી અદ્ભુત વાતો કેહેવાએલી છે. પણ એ અજાએબ સરખી વાતોને ટેકો આપવાને જરા પણ સાબિતી નથી. અને ખચીત એવું સાફ માલુમ પડેછે કે મહમદના જન્મ્યાને ઘણો કાળ ગયા પછી એવી વાતો કેહેવાવા માંડી. જો આવી અજાએબ જેવી અને પ્રગટ વાતો બની હોત તો એ વાતો લોકોને યાદ રેહેત, અને એથી તેઓ મહમદની કેહેણ કબુલ રાખત. ને લોકોએ મહમદને પુછ્યું કે કાંઈ ચમત્કાર કરી દેખાડે તો તું ઈશ્વરથી આવેલો છે એવું અમે માનીએ, તારે મહમદ પોતાના જનમ વેળાએ થએલા ચમત્કારો વિશે બોલ્યો હોત, પણ તેણે એમ કદી કીધું નહીં.

[૧] ખદીજા નામની કોરેષ જાતનીજ એક બાઈડી હતી. તે મક્કા શેહેરમાંના એક મોટા માણસની વીધવા હતી. તેને તાંહાં મહમદ પચીસ વર્ષની ઉમરે ચાકર રહ્યો. તેની ચાકરીમાં હતો તારે તે તેનાં ઉંટ અને તેનો વેપારનો માલ લઈને દમાસ્કસ શેહેરનાં મોટાં બજારમાં ગયો હતા. તેના ચિત્તાકર્ષક ગુણને લીધે આ સ્ત્રીને મહમદ એટલો તો પસંદ પડયો કે તેણે તેની સાથે લગન કીધાં. આ લગન થયાથી મહમદની અવસ્થા તેના જન્મ તથા કુળને યોગ્ય એવી થઈ. આવી દીશામાં આવ્યો તારે પોતાના ઘરડા વરડાઓ પોતાની જાતમાં મોટા સરદારો હતા, એ વાત તેને યાદ આવે, એમાં કાંઈ અશ્ચર્ય નહીં. પોતાના લગન થયા પછી તેણે પરદેશ ફરવું છોડી દીધું નહીં. પરદેશ ફરવાથી જુદા જુદા ધર્મ માનનારા જુદી જુદી પ્રજાના લોકોને તેણે જોયા, તેથી કરીને આગળ પાછળના દેશમાંના ધર્મના તથા રાજ્ય પ્રકરણના વિચારો તથા ધારાઓ વિશે તેને ગનાન મલ્યું. તે ગનાનનો તેણે પોતાના એકાંતના વિચારમાં ઉપયોગ કર્યો.

[૨] મહમદની પચીસથી તે ચાળીસ વર્ષની ઉમર સુધી

માં* કાંઈ મોટી જાણવા લાએક બીના બની નથી. તોપણ દુનિઆ ઉપર એક નવો ધર્મ સ્થાપવાનો હિંમત ભરેલો વિચાર તેણે જે કીધો તે આ અવસરમાં કીધો. માટે તેની જીંદગીમાં સઉ કર્ત્તાં આ મુદ્દત વધારે અગત્યની છે. પણ તેના મનમાં એ વિચાર કેમ આવ્યો, એ વિચાર આવ્યા પેહેલાં તેને શા શા વિચારો આવ્યા હતા, તેથી તેણે શું મતલબ હાંસલ કરવાની† ધારી હતી, તથા તે કેમ બહાર પડયો, એ વાતો આપણને બરાબર માલુમ નથી.

ઘણા વર્ષસુધી વિચાર કર્યા પછી પોતાની સઘળી યોજનાઓ પાકી કરીને, (ઈ૦ સ૦ ૬૦૯) મહમદ હળવે હળવે અને ઘણીજ ખબરદારીથી તે યુક્તિઓ પ્રમાણે કામ કરવા લાગ્યો. મક્કા શેહેરની પાસે હીરા નામની એક ગુફા હતી, તેમાં અપવાસ, ભક્તી, અને ઈશ્વર સંબંધી વિચાર કરવાને મહમદ કેટલીએક વારસુધી રોજ જયા કરતો. પોતે એકાંતમાં હતો તે વેળાએ જે કાંઈ અલૌકિક દેખાવો દીઠા અને વાણીઓ સાંભળી તેની વાતો તેણે સાંઝરે ઘેર આ-

---

* The words from *te* to *mañ* are all considered as one, 'in the "to-the-40th-year-of-his-life (time)."'

† Supply *āsā*, 'hope,' or some similar word.

વીને પોતાની બાઈડીની આગળ કેહેવા માંડી. આખરે તેણે પોતાની બાઈડીને કાંઈ વચન કહ્યું, અને તેને કહ્યું કે, એ વચન જબ્રીયેલ્ દૂતે આવીને મને ઈશ્વરી પ્રગટપણું આપેલું છે, તેમાંનો એક ભાગ છે. મહમદ એવું કેહેછે કે અલ્-કદ્ર એ નામની* રમઝાન મહિનાના ૨૩ મા તથા ૨૪ મા રોજની પ્રખ્યાત રાતે તે દુતે ચળકાટ ભરેલા આકારમાં આવીને મને સારા સમાચાર કહ્યા તે આ પ્રમાણે કે, "ઓ મહમદ તું ઈશ્વરનો મોકલેલો છે, અને હું જબ્રીયેલ્ દૂત છું." તે દૂતે રેશમી કાપડ દેખાડ્યૂં, તે ઉપર કાંઈ લખેલું હતું, અને વળી કહ્યું કે, "વાંચ." તે વેળાએ પેગંમબરે એમ ઉત્તર દીધો કે મારાથી વંચાતું નથી.† તારે દૂતે ફરીથી કહ્યું કે, "તારો પ્રભૂ જેણે સર્વે વસ્તુઓ ઉત્પન્ન કરીછે, અને જેણે માણસને બંધાઈ ગએલા લોહીનો બનાવેલો છે, તેનું નામ લઈને વાંચ. તારો દયાળુ પ્રભૂ, જેણે કલમ‡ પકડતાં સિખવું છે, અને જે વાતોથી માણસ અજાણો છે

---

* Feminine because agreeing with *rāt*, in the next line but one.

† Vide Gram., Cap. V. § 12 and § 13, pp. 67 and 70.

‡ "Through whom holding the pen must be learned." Vide Gram., Cap. V. § 4, fin. (p. 61.)

તે વાતો તેને સમજાવેછે, તેના નામથી તું વાંચ."*
જારે આવી અજાએબ સરખી મુલાકાતની વાત મહ-
મદે ખદીજાને કહી, તારે તેણે તે માની, અને એમ
કહ્યું કે, મહમદ કોઈ દાહાડો પોતાના લોકોનો પેગં-
મબર થશે. જે વાત ખદીજાએ સાંભળી તે વાત
તેણે તરતજ પોતાના વરકા નામના સગાને કહી.
તેણે પણ તે વાત માની, પણ તે મહમદના ચેલા-
ઓમોં ગણાએલો નથી.

પછી મહમદ સાધુસહી જીંદગી, જે પવિત્ર મના-
યછે, તેવી જીંદગીમાં રહેવા લાગ્યો. ને થોડા દાહા-
ડામાં તેનો એક ચાકર ઝૈદ ઈબન હારેથ નામે તેનો
ચેલો થયા. ઝૈદના ઈમાનને લીધે મહમદે તેને
સ્વતંત્રતા પાછી આપી; અને તારથી મુસલમાનોમાં
એવો ધારો પડયો છે કે જે ગુલામો મહમદનો ધર્મ
કબૂલ કરે તેઓને છુટા કરવા; તોપણ આ ધારો
સઘળી વેળા પળાયો નથી.

એ પ્રમાણે મહમદના મતનાં પેહેલવેલાં માન-
નારાં† તેની બાઈડી અને તેનો ગુલામ એ બે જણાં
હતાં.

---

* Suratu'l 'Alaq (Sura 96, vv. 1–5).

† Neut. because qualifying two nouns of dissimilar gender: Gram., Cap. III. § 2.

તેના ધરમમાં ત્રીજો માણસ જે આવ્યો તે તેના કાકા અબૂતાલેબનેા દીકરો અલી હતો. તે તે વેળાએ છોકરેા હતેા. ચોથો અબૂ-બકર નામનો મોટો આબરૂદાર અને મક્કા શેહેરમાં મોટી સત્તાદાર* માણુસ તેના ધરમમાં આવ્યો. અબૂ-બકરના સમજાવવાથી ઓથમાન, અબ્દુલ્-રેહેમાન્, સાદ, અલ્-ઝોબૈર, વગેરે કેટલાએક મક્કા શેહેરના મુખી માણુસો પણ આવ્યા. તેના ધરમમાં આ લોકો આવ્યા તે તેના અધીકારને મુખી ટેકો આપનારા અને બાહાદૂર લડવૈયા થયા. આ વેળાએ અબૂ-બકરે જે મદદ આપી તેને સારૂ મહમદે તેને અબ્દુલ્લાહ (ઈશવરનો દાસ), અલ્-સિદ્દીક (સાચો) અને અતીક્ એટળે બચેલો (નરકમાંથી) એવા ખતાબો તેને આપ્યા.

કોરેશ જાતના લોકો સામા થશે એવું ભય પામીને મહમદે ત્રણ વર્ષે સુધી પોતાના ધરમનો ઉપદેશ ખાનગી રીતેજ કર્યા કીધો. આ વેળાએ તેને ધણીએક ઈશવરી વાતો મળી, એવું મહમદ કેહેતો હતો. આખરે તેને અબૂ-બકરની મદદમાં પક્કો

---

* Fem. to qualify *sattā* in *sattādār*.

ભરોસો બેઠો, અને એવું જોયું કે હવે મારા ધરમના માનનારા ઘણા થયા છે, તારે ઈશવરે મને તમારી પાસે મોકલ્યો છે, અને તેની કેહેણ કેહેવાનો હુકમ કરેલો છે, એવું પોતાના સગાંવાહાલાંઓની આગળ કેહેવાનો તેણે ઠરાવ કીધો. પછી એ મતલબ સર તેણે તેના કાકાના છોકરા અલીને એક મજલસ કરવાનો હુકમ કીધો, અને તે મજલસનાં ઈજન અબ્દુલ્-મોતાલેબથી ઉતરેલાં સગળા માણસોને મોકલ્યાં. તેઓમાંના આસરે ચાળીસ જણે ઈજન કબૂલ રાખ્યાં. પછી તે ઈજન ફરીથી ફેરવ્યાં, અને ફરીથી કબૂલ થયાં તારપછી મહમદે તેઓને આ રીતે ભાષણ કીધું:—"જઝીરાત ઉલ-અરબમાં કોઈ એવો માણસ નહીં હશે કે જે ઠરાવ હમણાં હું મારાં સગાંઓને કેહેવા માગુંછું તેથી સારો ઠરાવ કરશે. હું તમને આ દુનિઆનું અને આવતી દુનિઆનું સુખ આપુંછું. સર્વશક્તિમાન ઈશવરે તમને તેની તરફ બોલાવવાનો મને હુકમ કરેલો છે, માટે તમારામાંથી મારો વઝીર (પ્રધાન) અને મારો ભાઈ કોણ થશે?"

તેઓ સગળાઓએ આનાકાની કરી, અથવા ના

કહી. તારે અલી ઉઠીને આ પ્રમાણે બોલ્યો—"ઓ ઈશવરના પેગંમબર! હું તારેા વઝીર થઈશ. જે માણસો તારી સામાં થશે તેના દાંત હું તોડી પાડીશ; તેના ડોળા હું ખેંચી કાઢીશ, તેનું પેટ હું ચીરી નાંખીશ, અને તેના ટાંટીઆ ભાગી નાંખીશ!" એવું અલીએ કહ્યું, તારપછી મહમદ તેને ઘણી નરમાશથી* ભેટયો, અને તે વેળાએ જેઓ આગળ હતા તેઓને આ પ્રમાણે કહ્યું—"આ મારો ભાઈ, મારો કારભારી, અને મારો ખલીફો છે, માટે તમે એને સ્વાધીન થઈને એને તાબે રેહો." તે વેળાએ સગળી મજલસ માત્ર તેની ઉપર હશી, અને અબૂ-તાલેબને કહ્યું, "હવે તારે તારા દિકરાને તાબે થવું જોઈએ."

એ પછી મહમદે લોકોમાં ખુલી રીતે ઉપદેશ કરવા માંડયો. તેની તીક્ષ્ણબુધી, કલ્પના, અને યાદદાસ્ત, પ્રવાસ કીધાથી તથા એકાંતી વીચાર કીધાથી સારી થઈ હતી, અને તેના શરીરની ખુબસૂરતી તથા બોલવાની મીઠાસ એવી હતી કે સગળા લોકોની તેના ઉપર મેહેરબાની થાય. પણ તેઓના મુરતી પુજક ધરમનો તથા તેમની હઠનો તેણે એટલો તો

* For the const. see Gr., Cap. V., § 10, note *.

તીરસ્કાર કીધો કે તેથી ઘણા ખરા લોકો તેના દુશમન થયા.

કેટલાએક લોકોએ તેને જાદુગર કહ્યો, કેટલાએકોએ તેને અસલની કાહાણીઓ કેહેનારો કહ્યો, અને કેટલાએકોએ સાફ રીતે તેને જુઠું બોલનાર તથા ઢોંગી કહ્યો. આ વખતે લોકોએ મહમદને માઠા અને જેથી ધિક્કાર થાય તેવા શબ્દ કહ્યા. એ વિશે કુરાનમાં ઘણીએક જગો પર લખેલું છેઃ—"મક્કાવાળા કેહેછે, ઓ જેને ચતવણી (કુરાન) મોકલેલી છે તે, તને ખરેખરૂં ભુત વળગેલું છેઃ જો તું ખરૂં બોલતો હોત તો શું તારી સાથે દુતો આવ્યા ન હોત? જવાબ, વાજબી વખત શીવાએ હમે દુતોને નીચે મોકલતા નથી." (કુરાન અ૦* ૬.) "તેઓ કેહેછે કે આ જાદુ છે, અને તે પર હમે વીશવાસ કરતા નથી; અને તેઓ કેહેછે જો આ કુરાન મક્કા તથા મદીના શેહેરોના કોઈ મોટા માણસને અપાયું હોત તો હમે તેને અંગીકાર કરત." (અ૦ ૪૩.) "મક્કાના લોકોને પોતાનો હીસાબ આપવાનો સમે પાસે આવેછે. પ્રભુથી તેઓને કાંઈ ચેતવણી આવતી નથી,

---

* અ૦ stands for અધ્યાય, 'chapter,' *i.e.* Sūra of the Qur'ān.

પણ જારે તેઓ સાંભળેછે તારે તેને તેઓ હશી કાહાડેછે. તેઓ કેહેછે કે, કુરાન એ સ્વપણાંનો ઢગલો છે, એટલુંજ નહીં, પણ તેણે જુઠાણું ચલાવેલું છે." (અ. ૨૧) "અને કાફર લોકો કેહેછે કે, કુરાન તેનું યોજેલું જુઠાણું છે, અને તે બનાવામાં તેને બીજાઓએ મદદ કરી છે, પણ તેઓ ગેરવાજબી વાત અને જુઠું બોલેછે. તેઓ એવું પણ કેહેછે કે, આ જુની કથાઓ છે, અને તેણે એ લખાવી છે, અને એ કથાઓ સાંઝે અને સવારે તેણે લખાવેલી છે. કહો કે, જે પૃથવી પરની તથા સ્વગમાંની છાની વાતો જાણેછે તેણે એ પ્રસિધ્ધ કરી છે. તેઓ કેહેછે કે, એ કઈ જાતનો મોકલેલો છે? તે આપણી પઠેજ ખોરાક ખાયછે, અને રસ્તાઓમાં ફરેછે. નાપાક લોકો એવું પણ કેહેછે કે, જે માણસને તમે માનોછો તે દીવાના શીવાએ બીજો કોઈ નથી." (અ૰ ૨૫.) "અવીશવાસીઓને જારે આપણે સાબિતીની નિશાણીઓ બતાવીએ છઈએ તારે તેઓ સાચાઈ વિશે કેહેછે કે એ તો જાદુ છે. તેઓ શું એમ કેહેછે કે મહમદે એ જુઠાપણું ચલાવ્યું? જવાબ, જો મેં એ જુઠાણું ચલાવ્યું છે તો ખરેખાત તમને મારે લીધે

ઈશવરથી મેહેરબાની મળશે નહીં: તમે તે વિશે કેવું ખરાબ બોલો છો એ તે સારીપઠે જાણેછે. જે મને પરગટ કરાએલું છે તે શીવાએ બીજું કાંઈ હું કેહેતો નથી; અને હું સઉને ખુલી ખબર આપનાર કરતાં વધારે નથી." (અ૰ ૪૬.)

પોતાનું મોકલેલાપણું ખરૂં બતાવવાને સઉથી મોટા ઈશવરનું નામ પણ દાખલ કીધું. "જે તમે દેખોછો, અને જે તમે નથી દેખતા, તેના સોગન્દ ખાઈને હું કહુંછું કે હું તમને જે કહુંછું તે આબરૂદાર મોકલેલાની વાતો છે, કાંઈ કવીની વાતો નથી: તમે કેટલો થોડો વીશવાસ લાવોછો! એ કાંઈશુકન જોનારની વાતો પણ નથી; તમે કેટલી થોડી ચેતવણી પામોછો! સગળા પ્રાણીનો જે પ્રભુ તેની પાસેથી એ પ્રગટપણું છે. જો આપણા વિશે જે વાતો કહી તેમાં મહમદે કાંઈ જુદાણું ચલાવ્યું હોત તો અમે તેનો જમણો હાથ પકડીને તેના અંતઃકરણની નસ કાપી નાંખી હોત." (કુરાન અ૰ ૪૯.) "કુરાનને હશી કાહાડવાને જે તીરસ્કાર ભરેલું બોલ્યો છે તે શ્રાપિત થાઓ. હું તેને નરકમાં બળવાને નાંખીશ." (અ૰ ૭૪.) "અવીશવાસીઓને સારૂ અમે સાંકળ,

બેડી, અને બળતી અગની, એ તૈયાર કર્યાં છે." (અ૰ ૧૧.)

મહમદ સઉથી ઘણો ગભરાયો એથી કે લોકોએ તેને વારે વાર પુછ્યા કીધું કે, તું ઈશવરથી આવેલો છે, એની સાચાઇ કાંઈ ચમતકાર કરીને સાબિત કર. તેના સાંભળનારાઓ કેહેવા લાગ્યા કે, "મુસા, ઈસા, અને બીજા પેગંમબરો તારા કેહેવા મુજબ ઈશવરના મોકલેલા છે, એવું સાબિત કરવાને ચમતકારો કરતા. હવે જો તું પેગંમબર હોય, અને તું અભીમાનથી કેહેછે તે મુજબ તારી આગળના પેગંમબરાથી મોટો હોય, તો અમને તારા પણ ચમતકાર જોવા દે. તું મુએલાને જીવતા કર, મુગાને બોલતા કર, અને બેહેરાને સાંભળતા કર; અથવા જવાહેરથી તથા કીમતી રાચરચીલાથી શોભાએમાન તારે સારૂ એક સોનાનો મેહેલ બનાવ; અથવા જે કિતાબ સ્વર્ગથી નીચે ઉતરેલી અથવા દૂતે તારી પાસે આણેલી તું કેહેછે તે અમને દેખાડ, એટલે અમે તારા ઉપર વીશવાસ કરીશું." આ સ્વભાવીક અને વાજબી સવાલો તેને કરતા તારે તે વાતો ઉડાવવાની તેણે ઘણીએક તદબીરો કીધી, એવું કુરાન ઉપરથી

માલુમ પડેછે. "કાફર લોક બોલેછે કે, ઈશવરનો મોકલેલો તું છે એની કાંઈ નિશાણી અમને બતાવશે, તાંહાં લગી અમે તારો વીશવાસ કરનાર નથી. પણ તને માત્ર ઉપદેશ કરનાર ઠેરવેલો છે, કાંઈ ચમતકાર કરવાને ઠેરવ્યો નથી." (કુરાન અ૦ ૧૩.) "જવાબ, નિશાણીઓ તો ઈશવરનાજ હાથમાં છે; અને હું પ્રગટ રીતે ઉપદેશ કરનાર છું, કાંઈ અધીક નથી." બીજી વખતે તે તેઓને કેહેછે કે, "જેઓએ આગળના પેગંમબરોના ચમતકારો દીઠા હતા તેઓએ તેમનો તીરસ્કાર કર્યો હતો, માટે હવે ઈશવર કાંઈ વધારે ચમતકાર કરશે નહિ. વળી જેઓને વીશવાસ કરવા સારૂ ઈશવરે ઠેરવ્યા છે તેઓ તો વગર* ચમતકારે વીશવાસ કરશે, પણ જેઓ એ પ્રમાણે પસંદ કીધેલા નથી, તેઓને ગમે એટલા ચમતકાર દેખાડીએ તોપણ તેઓ કબુલ કરનાર નથી." "અને જો તેઓની આગળ દૂતાને નીચે મોકલ્યા હોત અને મુએલાઓ તેઓની આગળ બોલ્યા હોત, તોપણ ઈશવરની ખુશી શીવાએ તેઓ વીશવાસ લાવત નહી," (અં૦ ૬.) તાર પછી જારે

* Or, more idiomatically, ચમત્કારના વગર.

મહીનામાં તે લશકરનો સરદાર હતો તારે એ હરકતોને દૂર કરવાને તેની પાસે એક જુદો રસતો હતો એ વેળાએ તે એવું કેહેતો હતો કે આગળ મુસાને તથા ઈસાને ચમતકાર કરવાની શકતી આપીને ઈશવરે મોકલ્યા હતા, તોપણ લોકો વીશવાસ લાવ્યા નહીં, માટે ઈશવરે હમણાં મને મોકલ્યો છે. હું જુદી તરેહનો પેગંમબર છું, અને તલવારના જોરથી વીશવાસ અણાવવાને મને ઠેરવ્યો છે.

મહમદના કેટલાએક વેહેમી શાગિર્દો કેહેછે કે, તેણે ચંદ્રના બે કડકા કીધા; ઝાડો તેને મળવા આવ્યાં; તેના હાથની આંગળીઓમાંથી પાણી વહ્યું; પથ્થરોએ તેને સલામ કરી; એક ભારવટીઓ તેની આગળ રડયો; એક ઉંટે તેની આગળ ફરીઆદ કરી; એક માંસના કકડાએ પોતે ઝેરી છે એવી તેને ખબર આપી. એવા એવા બીજા કેટલાએક ચમતકારો તેણે કીધા, પણ એ ચમતકારો વિશે મહમદ પોતે કાંઈજ બોલ્યો નથી, અને એવી વાતો કોઈ મોટા મુસલમાન કિતાબ લખનારાઓ પણ લખી ગયા નથી. વળી કુરાનમાં કેથે એ વાતો લખી નથી; તેમાં તો સાફ એમ કેહેછે કે મહમદ ચમતકાર વિના આવ્યો; એ ઉપરથી સાબિત થાયછે કે એ ચમતકારોની વાતો હમણાં થોડી મુદત ઉપરની બનાવટ છે.

II. MUḤAMMADAN INVASIONS OF INDIA.

હજરત મહમદ ઈ. સ. ૫૭૦ માં મક્કામાં જન્મ્યો હતો, અને તે મુસલમાન ધર્મનો સ્થાપનાર હતો. એણે પોતાનો ધર્મ આખા અર્બસ્તાનમાં ફેલાવ્યો, અને ઈ. સ. ૬૩૨ માં એના મરણ પછી એના ખલીફાઓએ એ ધર્મ સિરિયા, મિસર, ઈરાન, તુર્કસ્તાન અને અફગાનિસ્તાનમાં પ્રસાર કર્યો.

મહમદના મરણ પછી ૧૫ વરસે ઓસમાન નામના એક અરબે થાણા અને મુંબઈના કિનારા ઉપર એક દરિઆઈ કાફલો લૂટ મેળવવા માટે મોકલ્યો, પરંતુ તેમાં તેનું કાંઈ વળ્યું નહીં.

ઈ. સ. ૬૬૪ માં અરબ લોકો કાબુલ સુધી વધ્યા, અને ઈ. સ. ૭૧૨ માં બસરાના હાકેમના ભત્રિજા મહમદ કાસિમે સિંધ પર ચઢાઈ કીધી. આ વખતે સિંધમાં દાહીર નામે રાજા રાજ્ય કરતો હતો, અને તેની રાજ્યધાનીનું નામ દેવલનગર જેને હાલ કરાંચી કહેછે તે હતું. એ રાજાને કાસિમે હરાવી આખો સિંધ પ્રાંત જીતી લીધો, અને ત્યાંની વસ્તીનો નાશ કર્યો. દાહીર પણ લડતાં માર્યો ગયો. કાસિમની આ ફતેહ થયા છતાં તેની સત્તા નામનીજ રહી, અને થોડા વખતમાં તે જગ્યા રજપૂત લોકોએ પાછી

જીતી લીધી. હિંદુસ્તાનમાં જે મુસલમાન વંશે રાજ્યનો પાયો નાંખ્યો, અથવા જીતો મેળવીને પોતાની ખરી રાજ્યસત્તા સ્થાપી, તે ગિઝની વંશ હતો.

Establishment of the Ghaznavite Dynasty.

ઈ. સનની નવમી સદીમાં સેમેનીસ નામે ઓળખાતો તાતાર વંશ ખોરાસાનમાં રાજ્ય કરતો હતો, અને તેનું પાયતખ્ત બોખારા હતું. આ વંશના પાંચમા રાજા અબદુલ મલિકનો અલપ્તગીન નામે એક તુર્કી ગુલામ હતો, જે પાછળથી ખોરાસાનનો હાકેમ થયો; પણ રાજાનો કાળ થયાથી એ ગિઝનીમાં નાહાસી ગયો, જ્યાં તે ઈ. સ. ૯૭૬ માં સ્વતંત્રપણે રાજ કરવા લાગ્યો. એની પછી એનો ગુલામ તેમજ જમાઈ સબકતગીન ગિઝનીના રાજ્યનો ધણી થયો. એણે બલૂચિસ્તાન, તુર્કસ્તાન વગેરે મૂલકો જીતી પોતાનું રાજ્ય વધાર્યું. આથી લાહોરના રાજા જયપાળે એની ઉપર પેશાવર આગળ ઈ. સ. ૯૭૭ માં હુમલો કર્યો, પણ ત્યાંથી હાર ખાઈ તેને પાછું ફરવું પડ્યું. સબકતગીન હવે જયપાળ ઉપર વેર લેવાને પંજાબ ઉપર ચઢી આવ્યો. જયપાળની મદદે દિલ્હી, કનોજ, કલિંજર અને અજમેરના રાજાઓ આવ્યા હતા, પરંતુ તેમનો પરાભવ થયો. સબકતગીને સિંધુ નદી આગળની કેટલીક જગ્યા જીતી લીધી, અને

પુષ્કળ લૂટ મેળવી પાછો ગયો. સબક્તગીન તેની ૫૬ વરસની વયે ઈ. સ. ૯૯૭ માં મરણ પામ્યો, અને એની પાછળ એનો છોકરો મહમદ પોતાની ૩૦ વરસની વયે ગાદીએ બેઠો.

મહમદ ગિઝનવી ૯૯૭-૧૦૩૦—મહમદ પોતાના બાપની સાથે જયપાળ અને તેના મળતીઆઓ સામો ઘણી બાહાદુરીથી લડયો હતો. એના બાપના મરણ પછી એણે "સુલતાન" પદ ધારણ કર્યું. લૂટ મેળવવાના તથા પોતાનો ધર્મ હિંદુસ્તાનમાં ફેલાવવાના વિચારથી એણે આ દેશ પર ૧૨ સ્વારીઓ કરી. એ સ્વારીઓમાં એણે પુષ્કળ દોલત મેળવી, લાખોના જાન લીધા, અને લાખોને મુસલમાન કરી ગુલામ તરીકે વેચ્યા.

પેહેલી સ્વારી ૧૦૦૧ માં—એણે લાહોરના રાજા જયપાળ ઉપર કરી અને તેને પેશાવર આગળ હરાવી પકડયો. જયપાળે તેને ખંડણી આપવા કબુલ કરી ત્યારે તેને છોડયો. જયપાળ આ હારથી જે અપમાન પામ્યો હતો તે ન સહન થવાથી પોતાની ગાદી પર પોતાના છોકરા અનંગપાળને બેસાડી પોતે બળી મૂઓ.

બીજી સ્વારી ૧૦૦૪ માં—એણે મુલતાન પાસે ભાટીઆના રાજા વિજયરાય ઉપર કરી અને તેને હરાવ્યો, કારણ કે એ રાજા ખંડણી અટકાવી બેઠો હતો.

ત્રીજી સ્વારી ૧૦૦૫ માં—આ સ્વારી એણે મુલતાનના સરદાર અબ્દુલ ફ઼ાત લોદી સામે કરી તેને હરાવ્યો.

ચોથી સ્વારી ૧૦૦૮ માં—આ ચઢાઈ મહમદે લાહોરના રાજા જયપાળના છોકરા અનંગપાળ સામે કરી. એ રાજા દિલ્હી, કલિંજર, કનોજ અને બીજા રજપૂત રાજાઓ સાથે મળી જઈ સામો લડવા ગયો, પણ વૈહિંદગઢ આગળ હાર્યો. આ પછી મહમદે નગરકોટનું દેહેરૂં લૂટ્યું, જ્યાંથી પુષ્કળ દ્રવ્ય એને મળ્યું.

પાંચમી સ્વારી ૧૦૧૦ માં—આ સ્વારીમાં એણે મુલતાન જીતી લીધું, અને ત્યાંના સરદાર અબ્દુલ ફ઼ાત લોદીને કેદ કીધો.

છઠ્ઠી સ્વારી ૧૦૧૧ માં—સરસ્વતી અને જમના નદીની વચ્ચે થાણેશ્વર પર કરી અને બે લાખ હિંદુઓને કેદ કરી ગુલામો તરીકે વેચ્યા.

સાતમી તથા આઠમી સ્વારી ૧૦૧૪-૧૦૧૫ માં—આ વખતે મહમદ ગિઝનવીએ કાશ્મીર ઉપર ચઢાઈ કરી, પણ તેમાં એને સખત હાની થઈ અને માર ખાઈ પાછું જવું પડયું.

નવમી સ્વારી ૧૦૧૯ માં—આ સ્વારી એણે કનોજ ઉપર કરી. ત્યાંનો રાજા કુંવરરાય એની સામે લડયો નહીં, પણ એને તાબે થઈ દ્રવ્ય આપ્યું, તેથી મહમદે

તેને કાંઈ દુઃખ દીધું નહીં—ત્યાંથી મહમદ મથુરા ગયો. આ નગરમાં એણે વીશ દિવસ સુધી લૂટ ચલાવી અને ૫૩,૦૦૦ હિંદુઓને ગુલામ કરી બે બે રૂપિયે તેમને વેચ્યા.

દસમી તથા અગીઆરમી સ્વારી ૧૦૨૨-૨૩ માં—આ ચઢાઈ એણે કલીંજરના રાજા ઉપર કરી. આ વખતે અનંગપાળના છોકરા જયપાળ બીજાએ આ રાજાને મદદ કરી; તેનું પરિણામ એ નિપજ્યું કે મહમદે લાહોર ખાલસા કર્યું, અને ત્યાં રાજ્ય ચલાવવાને એક મુસલમાન સૂબો નિમ્યો. હિંદુસ્તાનમાં મુસલમાન રાજ્યની સ્થાપના આ વખતથી થએલી ગણાયછે. આગળ જોકે મુસલમાનોએ ચઢાઈ કરી ઘણીક જીતો મેળવી હતી ખરી, તોપણ હિંદુસ્તાનની એકે જગ્યાના તેઓ ધણી થયા ન હોતા.

બારમી સ્વારી ૧૦૨૪ માં—આ વખતે મહમદે પોતાની છેલ્લી ચઢાઈ ગુજરાતમાં સોમનાથ પર કરી, અને ત્યાંનું અતિ સુંદર દેહેરૂં લૂટયું. ત્રણ દિવસ સુધી લડાઈ ચાલી, અને જોકે તેનો બચાવ કરવાને ચામુંડનો પાટવીકુંવર વલ્લભસેન, તેનો ભત્રિજો ભીમદેવ, અને બીજા રજપૂત રાજા તથા સરદારો આવ્યો હતા, તોપણ આખરે મહમદ જીત્યો. આ દેહરૂં લગભગ સો વરસ સુધી ભાંગી હાલતમાં પડી

રહ્યું, અને પછી કુમારપાળ, જે ૧૧૬૬ માં મરણ પામ્યો, તેણે પાછું સમરાવ્યુ.

મહમદની મરજી ગિઝનીની ગાદી પોતાના પુત્ર મસુદને આપી ગુજરાતમાં પોતે રાજ કરવાની હતી; પણ લશ્કરના સરદારોના સમજાવ્યાથી તે વિચાર તેણે છોડી દીધો અને ત્યાં કોઈ પાદશાહી કુટુંબના બ્રાહ્મણને સૂબેા ઠરાવી ગિઝની જવા નિકળ્યો. અજમેરનેા રાજા એક મેાટા લશ્કર સહિત રસ્તેા રોકી બેઠેા છે તે સાંભળીને તેની સામે ન થતાં મહમદે સિંધનેા રસ્તેા લીધો. લશ્કરને રસ્તેા દેખાડનાર ભેામીયાનેા વેષ ધારણ કરી આવનાર સેામનાથનેા કોઈ બ્રાહ્મણ હતેા. તેણે મુસલમાનેા પર વેર લેવાને તેમને ત્રણ દિવસ અને રાત રણોમાં રખડાવ્યા જેથી તેમનાં હજારેા માણસ ખેારાક અને પાણી ન મળવાથી મરણ પામ્યાં. આખરે ઘણી મુશ્કેલીથી મહમદ ગિઝની જઈ પેાહોંચ્યેા.

મહમદ ગિઝનવી ઈ૦ સ૦ ૧૦૩૦ માં તેની ૬૩ વરસની વયે ગિઝનીમાં મરણ પામ્યો. એણે વિદ્યા અને હુન્નરને બહુ ઉત્તેજન આપ્યું. એના વખતમાં વિખ્યાત ઈરાની કવિ ફિરદેાસી થઈ ગયો. એના મરણ પછી ગિઝનીની ગાદીને માટે એના બે છેાકરા —મહમદ અને મસુદ—વઢયા, જેમાં મસુદે પેાતાના

ભાઈને આંધળો કર્યો, અને પછી રાજ્ય કરવા લાગ્યો. મસુદ પછી બીજા કેટલાક રાજાઓ થયા, જેઓ માંહેમાંહે વઢી નાશ પામ્યા, અને પંજાબ શિવાય સઘળી જગ્યા ખોઈ બેઠા. ગિઝનીની ગાદીએ ઈ૦ સ૦ ૧૧૧૫ માં છેલ્લો રાજા બેરામ હતો. એણે પોતાની છોકરી ઘોર વંશના એક રાજાને પરણાવી હતી. તેમની વચ્ચે કંઈ ભાંજગડ ઉઠવાથી બેરામે પોતાના જમાઈને મારી નાંખ્યો. આથી મરનારના ભાઈ અલાઉદ્દીન ઘોરીએ એના રાજ્યમાં મોટા લશ્કર સાથે કુચ કરી, અને ગિઝની જે મહમદે હિંદુસ્તાનની મેળવેલી લૂટોથી બહુ રળિયામણું કરી નાંખ્યું હતું તે સાત દિવસ સુધી લૂટી બાળી નાંખ્યું, ૧૧૫૨. આ ઉપરથી અલાંઉદ્દીન "જહાંસૂઝ" એટલે દુનિયા બાળનારના નામથી ઓળખાવા લાગ્યો. બેરામ હિંદુસ્તાન નાસી આવવા નિકળ્યો, પણ રસ્તામાંજ મરણ પામ્યો. બેરામ પછી એના છોકરા ખુસરૂ, અને પછી એના પૌત્ર ખુસરૂમલેકે લાહોરમાં રાજ્ય કર્યું. આ પછી અલાઉદ્દીન ઘોરીના ભત્રિજા શાહબુદ્દીન અથવા મહમદ ઘોરીએ તેના હાથમાંથી લાહોર પણ જીતી લીધું. આ પ્રમાણે ગિઝની વંશની સમાપ્તિ થઈ ઈ૦ સ૦ ૧૧૮૬.

The Ghori Dynasty.

અલાઉદ્દીન ઘોરીના ભત્રિજા શાહબુદ્દીન અથવા મહમદ ઘોરીએ ગિઝની વંશના છેલ્લા પાદશાહ ખુસરૂ મલેક પર ૧૧૮૬ માં ચઢાઈ કરીને લાહોર જીતી લીધું. આ વખતે હિંદુસ્તાનમાં ચાર મોટાં રજપૂત રાજ્યો હતાં—દિલ્હીમાં તુવાર, અજમેરમાં ચોહાણ, કનોજમાં રાઠોડ, અને ગુજરાતમાં વાઘેલા વંશના રજપૂતો રાજ્ય કરતા હતા. દિલ્હીના તુવાર રાજાને કંઈ સંતાન ન હોવાથી તેણે અજમેરના કુંવર પૃથુરાજને દત્તક કરી લીધો, જેથી પૃથુરાજ દિલ્હી તેમજ અજમેરના રાજ્યનો ધણી થયો. જ્યારે મહમદ ઘોરીએ દિલ્હી ઉપર ૧૧૯૧ માં ચઢાઈ કરી, ત્યારે આ પૃથુરાજ તેની સામો થયો અને તેને પાણીપતના મેદાનમાં હરાવ્યો. આ પછી રજપૂતો માંહોમાંહે લડી ઘણા નબલા પડી ગયો. કનોજના રાજાનો કુંવર જયચંદ, જે પૃથુરાજનો મસીઆઈ ભાઈ હતો, તેણે પૃથુરાજની અદેખાઈ કરી, અને તેની સામે લાંબો વખત સુધી લડયો. મહમદ ઘોરી ૧૧૯૧ માં હાર ખાધા પછી ગિઝની ગયો હતો, તે રજપૂતોને નબળા થઈ ગયલો જોઈ ૧૧૯૩ માં એક મોટાં લશ્કર સહિત પાછો હિંદુસ્તાન પર ચઢી આવ્યો. પૃથુરાજ પાછો એની સામો થયો; પણ ૧૧૯૩

માં સ્થાનેશ્વરના મેદાનમાં એ હારી ગયો ને દુશ્મનના હાથમાં પકડાયો, જેણે એને મારી નંખાવ્યો. ત્યાર પછી મહમદે અજમેર લૂટ્યું, અને એના ગુલામ કુતુબુદ્દીનને ત્યાંનો સૂબો નિમી એ પાછો ગિઝની ગયો. એક વરસ પછી પાછી હિંદુસ્તાન ઉપર એણે ચઢાઈ કરી, અને કનોજ તથા બનારસ જીતી લીધાં. કનોજના રાઠોડ રજપૂતો મારવાડમાં નાસી ગયા અને ત્યાં તેઓએ રાજ્ય ચલાવ્યું. મહમદ ઘોરીએ આ પછી ગુજરાત, અયોધ્યા, બંગાળા, અને બહાર જીતી લીધા. એણે હિંદુસ્તાન પર બંધી* મળી ૯ સ્વારીઓ કરી. ઈ. સ. ૧૨૦૬ માં ગિઝની જતાં પંજાબની ઉત્તર તરફના ગખકર નામે ઓળખાતી એક પાહાડી જાતના કેટલાક લોકોએ એના તંબુમાં ઘુસી જઈ એને મારી નાંખ્યો. એના મરણથી ઘોરી વંશની સમાપ્તિ થઈ.

III. AKBAR.

હુમાયૂંનો છોકરો અકબર ઈ. સ. ૧૫૪૩ માં અમરકોટમાં જન્મ્યો હતો. એનું ખરૂં નામ જલાલુદ્દીન હતું. એ પોતાના જન્મથી તે ઈ. સ. ૧૫૫૫ સુધી કંદહાર અને કાબુલમાં રહ્યો હતો. જ્યારે

* 'All united,' *i.e.* in all, altogether.

હુમાયું મરણ પામ્યો, ત્યારે એ માત્ર ૧૩ વરસની વયનો હતો. આ કારણને માટે પાંચ વરસ સુધી સઘળો રાજકારભાર એના પ્રધાન બેરામે ચલાવ્યો. સિકંદર સુર અને મહમદ આદિલશાહનો વજીર હેમુ અકબરની સામે લડવાને એક મોટું લશ્કર લઈ ગયા. પેહેલાં હેમુએ કેટલીક જગ્યા ઘણી બાહાદુરીથી લડાઈ કરીને જીતી લીધી, પણ પાછળથી પાણીપતના મેદાનમાં બેરામે તેને હરાવ્યો, અને મારી નાંખ્યો ઈ. સ. ૧૫૫૬. સિકંદર પણ થોડા વખતમાં અકબરને તાબે થયો. ઈ. સ. ૧૫૬૦ માં અકબરે પોતાના પ્રધાનના હાથમાંથી ૧૮ વરસની વયે સઘળી સત્તા છીનવી લીધી, કારણ કે એ ગર્વિષ્ટ અને તીખા સ્વભાવનો થયો હતો એટલુંજ* નહીં પણ પોતાની સત્તાનો ગેરઉપયોગ કરવા લાગ્યો હતો. બેરામે પોતાની સત્તા ખોવાથી એક બંડ ઉઠાવ્યું, પણ અકબરે તુરત તે બેસાડી દીધું. આ પછી બેરામ મક્કે† જવા નિકળ્યો પણ ગુજરાતમાં તેને મુબારકખાં નામના કોઈ પઠાણે મારી નાંખ્યો ઈ. સ. ૧૫૬૦.

ખાનઝેમાન, રાજબાહાદુર, આદમખાં, અબદુલ ખાં અને બીજા ત્રણ મુસલમાન સરદારો અકબરની સત્તા સામા થયા, અને બંડ ઉઠાવ્યાં. અકબર એ

---

* V. Gr., Cap. VI., § 3. † V. Gr., Cap. VI., § 5, p. 82.

સઘળા સામે સાત વરસ સુધી લડયો, અને તેમને વશ કર્યા (૧૫૬૦—૧૫૬૭).

આ પછી આ પાદશાહ જેપુરના રાજા ભારમલ, ઉદેપુર (ચિતોડ) ના સંગ રાજાના છોકરા ઉદયસિંગ, અને જોધપુરના રાજા માલદેવ જોડે ૧૫૬૭—૧૫૭૨ સુધી લડયો, અને ચિતોડ જીતી લઈ અકબર જોધપુરના રાજા માલદેવની છોકરી જોડે પરણ્યો. જાંહાંગીર આ રાણીનો કુંવર હતો. જેપુરના રાજા ભગવાનદાસે પણ અકબરને કન્યા દીધી. આ રાજાએ તેમજ તેના કુંવર માનસિંગે અકબરને તેના શત્રુઓને વશ કરવાને ઘણી મદદ આપી, અને તેઓ આ પાદશાહથી બહુ માન પામ્યા. અકબરે સઘળા રજપૂત રાજાઓને વશ કર્યા ખરા, પણ તેઓએ પાછળથી પોતાના રાજ્યનો ઘણો ખરો ભાગ જીતી લીધો, અને ઉદેપુર રાજધાની કરી.

અકબરે પોતાનાં* લાંબાં રાજ્યમાં ગએલી જગ્યાઓ પાછી જીતી લીધી અને ઘણી નવી જીતો મેળવી.

૧૫૯૫—અકબરે અહમદનગર જીતવાને પોતાના છોકરા મોરાદ અને એના આગલા વજીર બેરામના છોકરા મિરજાખાંને મોકલ્યા, પણ ત્યાંની રાણી ચાંદબીબીએ ઘણી બાહાદુરીથી તે જગ્યાનો બચાવ

* For the nasal *ṅ* added to these two words, V. Gr., p. 31, note *.

કર્યો, અને મોરાદ અને મિરજાખાંના લશ્કરને મારી કાઢયું. આખરે ૧૫૯૯ માં જયારે એ રાણીનું તેણીના વેરીઓએ ખુન કર્યું, ત્યારે ત્યાંની થોડીક જગ્યા અકબરે જીતી લીધી, અને ચાંદબીબીના છોકરા નિઝામશાહને ગ્વાલિયરના કિલ્લામાં કેદ કર્યો; બાકીની થોડીક જગ્યા ત્યાંના હબસી વજીર મલીક-અંબરે પોતાના મરણ (૧૬૨૬) સુધી બચાવી રાખી. આ જગ્યા પણ આખરે અકબરના પૌત્ર શાહજહાંએ ૧૬૩૭ માં જીતી લીધી.

આ પ્રમાણે આ પાદશાહે પોતાની સત્તા ઘણી ફેલાવી, તેમજ પોતાની રૈયતને ઘણી સુખી કરી. બંધા મુસલમાન રાજાઓમાં એ ઉત્તમ રાજા હતો. એણે હિંદુઓ ઉપરનો જજીઆવેરો કાઢી નાંખ્યો, અને ધર્મને માટે કોઈને પીડા કરી નહીં. પોતે ઘણો ભણેલો હોવાથી દરેક જાતની વિદ્યાને એ ઉત્તેજન આપતો. એણે મેહેસૂલ લેવાની રીતમાં સુધારો કર્યો, હિંદુઓને તેમની લાયકી પ્રમાણે ઉંચા ઓહદા આપ્યા, ગેરવાજબી કરો કાઢી નાંખ્યા, અને સતી થવાની માઠી ચાલનો અટકાવ કર્યો. અકબરના વખતમાં ઘણાક મહાન પુરૂષો હતા, જેમાં મુખ્ય રાજા ટોડરમલ્લ નામે એક હિંદુ, જે મેહેસૂલ ખાતાનો વડો હતો તે, અને એ પાદશાહનો વજીર અબુલફઝલ જેણે "આઈને અકબરી" નામના

પુસ્તકમાં અકબરનું જન્મ ચરિત્ર લખ્યું છે, તેઓ હતા. અકબરને ત્રણ છોકરા હતા—(૧) સલીમ જેણે ૧૬૦૧ માં પોતાના બાપ સામેજ બંડ ઉઠાવ્યું હતું, અને જે અકબર પછી ગાદીએ બેઠો, (૨) મોરાદ જે ૧૫૯૯ માં મરણ પામ્યો, અને (૩) દાનિયાલ જે ૧૬૦૪ માં મરણ પામ્યો. એનો વડો પુત્ર સલીમ સારી ચાલનો ન હોવાથી અકબરને ઘણું દુઃખ લાગતું, તોપણ મરતી વેળા એણે પોતાના સઘળા ઉમરાવોને બોલાવી તેમના* દેખતાં સલીમને રાજ્યનો વારસ ઠરાવ્યો, જેથી કરીને† કે એનાં મરણ પછી રાજ્યમાં ગાદી માટે કાંઈ બખેડા થાય નહીં. અકબર ઈ. સ. ૧૬૦૫ માં મરણ પામ્યો. એની લાસ આગ્રામાં દાટવામાં આવી હતી.

JAHĀNGĪR.

અકબરના વડા છોકરા સલીમે ગાદીએ બેસતાં જાંહાંગીર એટલે "દુનિયા જીતનાર" એવું નામ ધારણ કર્યું. એણે અહમદનગર, બિજાપુર અને ગોવળકોંડાના રાજ્યોપર હુમલો કરી ખંડણી લીધી, અને એના છોકરા શાહજાહાંએ ઉદેપુર ઉપર હુમલો

---

* 'In their presence,' 'when they were looking on.'

† 'With this object in view that,' *etc.*

કરી ત્યાંના રાણાને હરાવ્યો. આરંભમાં સલીમે એના બાપનાં કીધેલાં સર્વ કામો જારી રાખ્યાં, પણ પાછળથી તેમ કર્યું નહીં. ઈ. સ. ૧૬૧૧ માં જાંહાંગીર નુરજહાં સાથે પરણ્યો. નુરજહાં અયાઝ નામના કોઈ ગરીબ ઈરાની ઉમરાવની ઘણી રૂપાળી બેટી અકબરનાં જનાનખાનામાં તેણીની મા જોડે જતી. જ્યારે અકબર જીવતો હતો ત્યારે સલીમે તેને જોઈને તેની સાથે પરણવા માગ્યું, પણ અકબરે તેમ ન કરતાં તેને શીરઅફગાન નામના એક બાહાદુર હાકેમ સાથે પરણાવી. જ્યારે સલીમ ગાદીએ બેઠો ત્યારે તેણીની સાથે પરણવાના વિચારથી તેણીના ભરથારને તેણે સમજાવ્યો; પણ જ્યારે તેણે તેમ કરવા ના કહી ત્યારે જાંહાંગીરે તેને મારી નખાવ્યો. આથી નુરજહાં ઘણી ગુસ્સે થઈ, પણ આખરે થોડા વખતમાં તેણી સલીમ જોડે પરણી, અને તેણીના બાપ અને ભાઈને તેણીએ મોટી મોટી પદ્દીઓ અપાવી. સલીમને પોતાના છોકરાઓથી ભારે દુઃખ ખમવું પડ્યૂં હતું. એના વડા છોકરા ખુસરૂએ એની સામે બંડ ઉઠાવ્યૂં, પણ તે આ પાદશાહે તુરત બેસાડી દીધું, અને ખુસરૂને ગ્વાલિયરના કિલ્લામાં કેદ કર્યો, જ્યાં તે ૧૬૨૧ માં મરણ પામ્યો. એનો બીજો છોકરો પરવીઝ જેને એણે દક્ષિણનો સૂબો બનાવ્યો હતો તે ૧૬૨૬ માં મરણ પામ્યો. ઈ. સ. ૧૬૨૩ માં

એના બીજા છોકરા શાહજહાંએ પણ બંડ ઉઠાવ્યું, કારણ કે સલીમની મરજી પોતાના ચોથા છોકરા શહેરિયારને ગાદી આપવાની હતી.

ઈ. સ. ૧૬૨૫ માં નુરજહાંને મોહોબતખાં નામના એક અમીર જોડે કજીઓ થયો, કારણ કે એ અમીરે સલીમના બીજા છોકરા પરવીઝનો પક્ષ કર્યો હતો. નુરજહાંએ એનાપર ખોટી તોહોમતો મુકી એને ઘણો સતાવ્યો, તેથી આ અમીરે ૫,૦૦૦ રજપૂત સ્વારો લઈ સલીમને કેદ કર્યો ૧૬૨૬. નુરજહાંએ સલીમને છોડવવાના ઘણાક ઉપાયો લીધા, અને આખરે તેને છોડવ્યો. કેદમાંથી છુટયા પછી તે થોડા વખતમાં કાશ્મીરથી લાહોર જતાં તેની ૬૦ વરસની વયે ઈ. સ. ૧૬૨૭ માં મરણ પામ્યો. આ રાજાની દરબારમાં ઈ. સ. ૧૬૦૭ માં "કમ્પનીએ" કેપ્તન હોકિન્સ નામના એક ગૃહસ્થને મોકલ્યો હતો; અને પછી ઈંગ્લાંડના પેહેલાં જેમ્સ રાજા તરફથી અંગ્રેજી એલચી સર ટોમસ રો ૧૬૧૫ માં આવ્યો હતો. એ બન્નેને સલીમે પેહેલાં સારો આવકાર દીધો, પણ પાછળથી મોકિબખાં નામના સૂબાના, તેમજ નુરજહાંનો ભાઈ અસોફખાં જે વજીર થયો હતો તેના, અને સલીમના છોકરા શાહજહાંના સમજાવ્યાથી પાદશાહે તેમને દરબાર છોડી જવાનો હુકમ કર્યો.

સલીમ સમજણવાળો અને ઈનસાફી પણ દારૂ-

ઓ હતો. પોતાની રૈયતની ફરિયાદ પોતે સાંભળવાને માટે પોતાના ઓરડાની અંદરથી તે જમીન સુધી એક લાંબી સાંકળ રાખતો; જે સાંકળનો છેડો તેના મેહેલમાં હતો તેની સાથે ઘંટો બાંધેલા હતા; માટે જયારે કોઈ ફરિયાદ કરવા જતો, ત્યારે તે સાંકળ તે ખેંચતો, જેથી ઘંટોનો અવાજ થતો, અને પાદશાહ તે માણસને પોતાની આગળ બોલાવીને તેની ફરિયાદ સાંભળી લેતો.

AURANGZEB.

ઈ. સ. ૧૬૫૭ માં શાહજહાં ઘણો માંદો પડયો, ત્યારે દારા તેના બાપ પાસે આગ્રે હતો, સુજા બંગાળામાં, ઔરંગજેબ દક્ષિણમાં, અને મુરાદ ગુજરાતમાં હકુમત ચલાવતા હતા.

જયારે આ છોકરાઓએ પોતાના બાપના મંદવાડના સમાચાર સાંભળ્યા, ત્યારે સુજા અને મુરાદે ગાદીના ધણી થવાના વિચારથી પાયતખ્ત ભણી કુચ કરી. ઔરંબજેબ, ગોવળકોંડાના પ્રખ્યાત સરદાર મિરજુમલાને પોતાના પક્ષમાં લઈ, પોતાના બેવકુફ ભાઈ મુરાદ સાથે મળી ગયો, અને તેને સમજાવ્યું કે મારે તો મકકે જઈ ભકિત કરી મારો વખત કાઢવો છે; પણ હું એમ કરૂં તે પેહેલાં મારી ઈચ્છા તને ગાદી અપાવવાની છે, કારણ કે તારા શિવાય

બિજા ભાઈઓ રાજ્ય ચલાવવાને યોગ્ય નથી. મુરાદે ઔરંગજેબના બોલવા પર પૂર ભરોસો રાખ્યો, અને તેની સાથે મળી ગયો. પેહેલાં દારાએ પોતાના ભાઈ સુજાને ૧૬૫૭ માં કાશી આગળ હરાવ્યો; પણ ૧૬૫૮ માં ઔરંગજેબ અને મુરાદે દારાના સેનાપતિ જસવંતસિંહને પેહેલાં ઉજ્જેણ આગળ, અને પછી તેજ વરસમાં દારાને આગ્રા આગળ હરાવ્યો. એમ કહેછે કે દારાના હાથીને કંઈ લાગ્યાથી તે ઘણો મસ્તાન થયો, માટે દારા નીચે ઉતરી પડયો; પણ લશ્કરને તે વિષે કંઈ ખબર ન હોવાથી, તેમજ વળી હાથીને ખાલી જોવાથી, તેઓએ એમ વિચાર્યું કે દારા માર્યો ગયો—અને તેથી તેઓ સઘળા નાસી ગયા. દારા આગ્રા આગળ હારી ગયા પછી દિલ્હીમાં નાસી ગયો. ઔરંગજેબે આ ફતેહ મેળવ્યા પછી તુરત પોતાના બાપ સલીમને એક કિલ્લામાં પૂર્યો, અને દારાની પુઠે દિલ્હી ગયો. રસ્તે જતાં ઔગરંજેબે મુરાદને કેદ કર્યો, અને દિલ્હીમાં પોતાના નામની દુવાઈ ફેરવી ઈ. સ. ૧૬૫૮.

શાહજહાં ૧૬૬૮ માં બંદીખાને રહીને મૂઓ. તાજમેહેલ જે એક અતિ સુંદર ઈમારત છે, તે આ પાદશાહે પોતાની બેગમ મુમતાજમહાલની યાદગારી સારૂ બંધાવ્યો હતો.

ઔરંગજેબ અથવા આલમગિર પેહેલાએ પોતાના ભાઈઓને દગાથી તેમજ ખુલ્લી રીતે લડાઈઓ કરીને વશ કર્યા:—દારા જ્યારે મુલતાનથી નાસી જતો હતો, ત્યારે તેને ત્યાંના સૂબા જહાનખાંએ પકડી ઔરંગજેબ પાસે મોકલાવી આપ્યો, જેણે ૧૬૫૯ માં તેને મારી નંખાવ્યો. સુજા ૧૬૫૯ માં કજવાની લડાઈમાં હારી જઈ આરાકાન નાસી ગયો, જ્યાં તે ૧૬૬૦ માં મરણ પામ્યો; અને મુરાદને કંઈ બહાનું કાઢી ૧૬૬૧ માં મારી નાંખ્યો. આ પ્રમાણે એણે પોતાના હરીફોને મારી નાંખી "આલમગિર" અથવા દુનિયાં જીતનારનાં નામથી રાજ્ય ચિન્હો ધારણ કર્યાં. શાહજહાંને બંદીખાનેથી છોડવવાને જોધપુરના રાજા જસવંતસિંહે અને બીજા કેટલાકોએ યુક્તિઓ કરી હતી પણ તેમાં તેઓ ફાવ્યા ન હતા.

ઔરંગજેબે પોતાના બાપથી ઉલટી રીતે ચાલીને હિંદુઓ ઉપર ભારે વેરો નાંખ્યો, અને તેમનાં દેહેરાં લૂટી તેમના ઉપર ઘણી તરેહના ધર્મ સંબંધી જુલમો ગુજાર્યા. આથી તેનાં રાજ્યમાં શાંતી રહી નહીં. દિલ્હીની નૈરૃત્ય કોણે નારોળ ગામમાં સતરામી નામના હિંદુઓએ બંડ ઉઠાવ્યું, અને ઔરંગજેબનાં લશ્કરને ઘણીકવાર મારી હાંકી કાઢ્યું. આખરે જ્યારે એ રાજા પોતે એક લશ્કર લઈ ત્યાં

ગયો, અને તેમને હરાવ્યા, ત્યારે તેઓ તાબે થયા, ઈ. સ. ૧૬૭૬.

જોધપુરના રાજા જસવંતસિંહે ઔરંગજેબને હિમ્મતથી એક કાગળ લખી હિંદુઓપર જુલમ નહીં ગુજરવાને સમજાવ્યો; પણ આ પાદશાહે તે ઉપર કંઈ ધ્યાન આપ્યું નહીં, એટલુંજ નહીં, પણ ૧૬૭૭ માં જસવંતસિંહના મરણ પછી એ તેની સ્ત્રી અને બે કુંવરો ઉપર પણ જુલમ ગુજારવા લાગ્યો; આથી જેપુરનો રાજા રામસિંહ, મેવાડનો રાજસિંહ, અને બીજા ઘણાક રજપૂત રાજાઓ ઔરંગજેબની સામા* થયા. એમને વશ કરવાને પાદશાહે પોતાના છોકરા મોઆજીમ, આજમ, અને અકબરને એક મોટું લશ્કર આપી મોકલ્યા, જેઓએ તેમને હરાવી તેમના ઉપર બહુ જુલમ ગુજાર્યો. ઔરંગજેબે ૧૬૮૩—૧૭૦૭ સુધી દક્ષિણમાં લડાઈઓ ચલાવી અને ૧૬૮૬ માં સિકંદર આદિલશાહને હરાવીને બિજાપુર, ૧૬૮૭ માં અબુલહુસેનને હરાવીને ગોવળકોંડા, અને ૧૭૦૦ માં સતારા જીતી લીધાં. ઈ. સ. ૧૭૦૧ માં અંગ્રેજી એલચી સર વિલિયમ નોરિસે ઔરંગજેબની ભેટ લીધી હતી. આ પાદશાહે પોતાની સત્તા છેક કન્યાકુમારિ સુધી ફેલાવી, અને જમાબંધીની ઉપજના ૩૬

* Notice that this *adj. sāmo* requires the *fem. gen.* (*-nī*) before it

કરોડ રૂપિયા વસુલ કર્યા. એના જુલમને લીધે રજપૂતો, જેઓ લાંબો વખત* થયો મોગલ વંશના રાજાઓના મિત્ર હતા, અને લડાઈને વખતે તેમને મદદ કરતા, તે લોકો તેમજ મરેઠા લોકો એના કટ્ટા વેરી થયા, જેમને એ મરણ પામ્યો† ત્યાંસુધી વશ કરી શકયો નહીં. ઔરંગજેબ ૧૭૦૭ માં અહમદનગરમાં પોતાની ૮૯ વરસની વયે મરણ પામ્યો.

ઔરંગજેબને પાંચ શાહજાદા હતા—મહમદ જે ૧૬૬૭ માં ગ્વાલિયરમાં મરણ પામ્યો, મોઆજીમ, અકબર, આજમ, અને કામબક્ષ. મોઆજીમ શાહઆલમ પેહેલાના નામથી ગાદીએ બેઠો. આજમ એની સામો થયો, પણ ૧૭૦૭ માં આગ્રા આગળની લડાઈમાં માર્યો ગયો. કામબક્ષ પણ મોઆજીમ સામો લડવા ગયો પણ ૧૭૦૮ માં હૈદ્રાબાદની લડાઈમાં માર્યો ગયો.

IV. ḤAIDAR 'ALĪ.

હૈદર ઈ. સ. ૧૭૦૨ માં જન્મ્યો હતો. એ મ્હૈસૂરમાં હિંદુ રાજાના ઘોડે‡ સ્વાર લશ્કરના એક અમલદારનો છોકરો હતો. મ્હૈસૂરના રાજાની નોકરીમાં

---

* 'For a long time since.'

† 'Up to the time he died,' *i.e.* 'as long as he lived.'

‡ 'Mounted on horseback.'

એ ૨૧ વરસની વયે દાખલ થયો. થોડા વખતમાં એ પોતાની ચાલાકીથી ઊંચી પદ્દીએ ચઢયો. લૂટ, લૂચ્ચાઈ, અને ઠગાઈથી એણે મોટું લશ્કર અને ઘણા પૈસા એકઠા કરી મ્હૈસૂરના પ્રધાન નન્દરાજ, જેના હાથ નીચે એ નોકરી કરતો હતો, તેને દૂર કર્યો, અને રાજા તેમજ નન્દરાજને* વરસ દહાડ ચોકસ રકમ આપવા* કહીને પોતે મ્હૈસૂરનો ધણી થયો ઈ. સ. ૧૭૬૧. ૧૭૬૩ માં એણે બડનેારનો કિલ્લો લીધો. ચોથા પેશ્વા માધવરાવે એનું બળ ઘણું વધતું જોઈને એના ઉપર એક મોટું લશ્કર લઈ જઈ એને સખત હાર આપી, જેથી એને મરેઠાઓને ૩૨ લાખ રૂપિયા આપવા પડયા. ૧૭૬૬ માં એણે કાલિકટ જીત્યું. આ ફતેહથી નિઝામ અને મરેઠાઓએ સંપ કરી હૈદરનું સઘળું રાજ લઈ લેવાનો વિચાર કર્યો; પણ હૈદર તેમને લાંચ આપી બચી ગયો. હૈદરે હવે અંગ્રેજોનાં રાજ ઉપર હુમલો કર્યો, પણ કર્નલ સ્મિથે તેને ૧૭૬૭ માં ચંગામ અને ત્રિનોમાલી આગળ હરાવ્યો. અમ્બુરગઢ ઉપર પણ હુમલો કરવામાં હૈદર હારી ગયો. આવી હાર થયાથી એ એક મોટું લશ્કર લઈ કર્ણાટક પાયમાલ કરી છેક મદ્રાસ તરફ વધી ગયો અને અંગ્રેજી લશ્કરને મારી વિખેરી નાંખ્યું. આ ફતેહથી હૈદરે હવે મરેઠાની

---

* 'To give precisely a year and a day's allowance (of notice).'

જીુસરીમાંથી નિકળી જવાની તૈયારી કરી, પણ ઈ. સ. ૧૭૭૨ માં ચેરકુલીની લડાઈમાં મરેઠા સરદાર ત્રિંબ-કરાવે તેને સખત હાર ખવાડી, જેથી તેને મરેઠા-ઓને ૩૬ લાખ રૂપિયા અને કેટલીક જગ્યાઓ આપવી પડી. જ્યારે મરેઠાઓ એનાં રાજ્ય પર ચઢી આવ્યા ત્યારે એણે ૧૭૬૯ ની મદ્રાસની સંધિ પ્રમાણે અંગ્રેજોની મદદ માંગી, પણ તેઓએ તેનું કંઈ સાંભળ્યું નહીં; આથી હૈદર તેમનો કટ્ટો દુશ્મન થયો. મરેઠાઓની માંહોમાંહેની લડાઈથી હૈદરે પાંચ વરસમાં પોતાની ખોએલી સઘળી જગ્યા પાછી જીતી લીધી, અને એક ઘણું મોટું લશ્કર લઈ અંગ્રેજોની સામો પાછો ગયો. કર્નલ બેલી એની સામો લડવા આવ્યો, પણ પોલીલોરની પેહેલી લડાઈમાં તે હારી ગયો, અને કેદ પકડાયો ઈ. સ. ૧૭૮૦. ૧૭૮૧ માં આયરકૂટ સરદારે પોર્ટોનોવો અને પછી શોલિં-ગરની લડાઈમાં હૈદરને હરાવ્યો. હૈદરે ૧૭૮૨ માં તેલીચરિ ઉપર હુમલો કર્યો, પણ ત્યાંના રેહેવાસી-ઓએ બાહાદુરીથી ૧૮ માસ સુધી ટકાવ કર્યો, અને પછી મદદ મળતાંજ હૈદરનાં લશ્કર પર હુમલો કરી તેને હરાવ્યો, અને તેના ૧૨૦૦ માણસને બંદીવાન કીધાં. આ વગર ભણેલો પણ શૂરો માણસ ૧૭૮૨ માં પોતાની ૮૦ વરસની ઉમરે ચિતોડમાં મરણ પામ્યો.

V. EXTRACTS FROM A GUJARĀTĪ NEWSPAPER.

[These extracts are written in Pārsī-Gujarātī, but, except that (1) they contain a few more Arabic and Persian words than ordinary Gujarātī, (2) that *l* continually takes the place of *ḷ*, and *par-* of *pra-*, and (3) that *y* is occasionally omitted in the preterite of verbs, need little remark.* The English words and proper names which occur in them are not inserted in the Vocabulary. But, as the student may perhaps find them troublesome to recognise in their Gujarātī dress, we append a list of them here in the order in which they occur.

Freñch = French.
Yurop = Europe.
Vāisrāy = Viceroy.
Keneḍā = Canada.
Ḍepyuṭeśan = Deputation.
Frenchmen = Frenchman.
Lārḍ Grānvīl = Lord Granville.
Perīs = Paris.
Briṭiś = British.
Frāñs = France.
Eḍīnbaro Rīvyu = Edinburgh Review.
Mī. Henrī Rīv = Mr. Henry Reeve.
Ḍyuk ov Beḍforḍ = Duke of Bedford.
Sar Chārlas Ḍīlk = Sir Charles Dilke.
Seṭarḍe Rīvyu = Saturday Review.
Senṭsbarī = Saintsbury.
Lārḍ Sālsbarī = Lord Salisbury.
Lārḍ Rozbarī = Lord Roseberry.
Lārḍ Jyārj Hemilṭan = Lord George Hamilton.
Lārḍ Bīkansfīlḍ = Lord Beaconsfield.
Mājisṭreṭ = Magistrate.
Mī. Kupar = Mr. Cooper.
Polīs = Police.
Kāñsṭebal = Constable.
Nelmas = Nelmes.
Solīsiṭar = Solicitor.
Mī. Līṭal = Mr. Little.
Āspīṭal = Hospital.
Līsṭ = list.
K̇āronar = Coroner.
Seśans kamīṭ (karvuñ) = to commit to the Sessions.
Kalāke = o'clock.]

* But we may also notice that such phrases as (1) "*amo jatāñ hatāñ*" etc. for *ame jatā hatā*, and also (2) "*agarjo mane khabar* hate *to kaḍī bī huñ tyāñ* ... sute *nahī*," for *jo mane khabar* hot, *to kaḍī paṇ huñ tyāñ* ... *sutī na*hot, are Pārsī peculiarities. In the first phrase the verb is not *neuter* but *masc.* with a nasal sound attached.

1.—સફાઈદાર અને સુધ ફરેંચ ભાશા બોલનાર ઈંગરેજો.

ઈંગરેજો ફરેંચોના પાડોશી છે અને એકમેક સાથે વેપાર ધંધા વગેરેનો ઝાઝો સંબંધ હોવાથી તથા યુરોપમાં સંધે ફરેંચ ભાશા સાધારણ હોવાથી, ઘણા-ખરા ઈંગરેજો ફરેંચ શીખે છે પણ તે શુધ ઉચારે અને વયાકરણ કે રૂઢીની ભુલચુક વગર થોડાઓજ બોલી શકે છે અને તેઓ નવાઈના નમુના ગણાય છે. તેવાઓમાં એક આપણા નામદાર વાઈસરાય છે. તેવણ કેનેડાના વાઈસરાય હતા તે વખતે એક ફરેંચ ડેપયુટેશન તેમને માનપતર આપવા આવયું તેનો જવાબ આપતાં તેવણે એવી સરસ ફરેંચ ભાશા વાપરી કે પેહેલા બે તરણ બોલો તેમનાં મોહમાંથી બહાર પડતાંજ ડેપયુટેશનના ગરહસ—થોએ હરખના પોકાર કરવા માંડયા પણ તેવણના મમાવા ફરેંચમેન હતા અને તેથી ફરેંચની એ શુધતા તેવણમાં ઓધે ઉતરી છે. લારડ ગરાન-વીલ બી સારી છટાથી ફરેંચ બોલે છે. તેવણના પીતા પેરીસ ખાતે બરીટીશ એલચી તરીકે ઘણાં વરસ રહેલા હતા અને તેવણ જોડે લારડ ગરાનવીલે બી જવાનીનો ઘણો વખત ફરાંસમાં ગુજારયો હતો તથા વલી તેમની પેહેલી બાયડી બી જાતે ફરેંચ હતી.

આથી તેવણુને ફરેંચ ભાશા અને ફરેંચ પરજાનો ઘણો સરસ અનુભવ છે અને પરદેશખાતાંના પરધાન હતા તે વખતે એ અનુભવ તેમને બહુ કામ લાગો હતો. ઈંગલંડમાં તેવણ ફરેંચ ભાશાના ખાં ગણાય છે પણ તેવણ પોતે તે માન ના પાડી કહેછે કે તેમનું ભંડોલ ઊંડું નહી પણ બાહેરનું છે. વયાકરણનું શુધપણું, ઉચારની સફાઈ અને છટાદાર ઢપની મદદથી તેવણનું એ ભાશાનું થોડું જ્ઞાન દેખઈતું વધારે લાગેછે. પણ ઈંગરેજોમાં સઉથી સરસ ફરેંચ ભાશા બોલનાર એડીનબરો રીવયુનો અધીપતી મી૰ હેનરી રીવ કહેવાય છે. ડયુક ઓવ બડફરડ લગભગ એવાજ સરસ ફરેંચના ખાં છે, પણ તેવણ એવી ખુણે પડેલી જીંદગી ગુજારે છે કે તેમનાં ભંડોલનો લાભ દુનયાને મલતો નથી. સર ચારલસ ડીલક છટાથી અને શુધ ફરેંચ બોલે છે પણ તેમના ઉચારો મન માનતા નથી. "સેટરડે રીવયુ" નો અધીપતી મી૰ સેનટસબરી ફરેંચ બોલવામાં ઝાઝો કુશલ નથી પણ ફરેંચ સાહીતયનું ભંડોલ તેનામાં જબરૂં છે. લારડ સાલસબરી છટાથી ફરેંચ બોલે છે પણ ઉચાર અને જાતીમાં ઝૂરાબંધ ભુલો કરે છે, લારડ રોઝબરી ધીરે ધીરે અને સંભાલથી બોલે છે. લારડ જયારજ હેમીલટન ફરેંચ જાણતા નથી અને એ કારણને લીધે તો ૧૮૭૪માં લારડ બીકનસફીલડે તેવણને

પરદેશખાતાંનું નાયબ પરધાનપદ આપવા માગચું તે લેવા તેઓએ ના પાડી હતી.

2.—અંજાણપણે ખુન કરવાનો આરોપ.

ગઈ પરમ દીને વડા માજીસટરેટ મી૰ કુપર સનમુખ પોલીસ ફોજના કાનસટેબલ મી૰ નેલમસે નારાયણ કેવારી નામના એક ઘોડાવાલાને બેદરકારીથી ગાડી હાંકી ભાગી નામની એક છોકરીને કચડી નાંખી અંજાણપણે ખુન કરવાના આરોપ માટે ઉભો કરચો હતો. સરકાર તરફથી મુકદમો ચલાવવાને સરકારી સોલીસીટર મી૰ લીટલ હાજર હતા. * * * * *

આરોપીએ સાક્ષીને ઉલટપાલટ તપાસવાની ના પાડી હતી.

ભીમી નામની સ્ત્રીએ મી૰ લીટલની તપાસમાં જણાવચું કે હું ભીખ માગું છું. મરનાર મારી દીકરી થતી હતી. તેણીનું નામ ભાગી હતું. તેણીની ઉમર બે વરસની હતી. ધોબીતલાવ ઉપર આવેલી એક ચાલી આગલ એક દીવસે સવારનાં દશ કલાકે રોટી ખાઈ હું અને મરનાર સુતાં હતાં, એ વેલાએ બાજુ થવાની કશી ખુમ મારચા વીના, આરોપીની ગાડી તયાં દાખલ થઈ અને અમારા શરીર ઉપરથી પસાર થઈ ગઈ હતી. એ ચાલીના ઓટલાની બાજુની જમીન ઉપર અમો સુતાં હતાં. એ ગાડી મોટા

રસતા ઉપરથી દાખલ થઈ હતી. તે વેલાએ ફકત મારી આંખ લાગી હતી, હું સુઈ ગઈ ન હતી. જ્યારે મારી દીકરીએ (મરનારે) ચીચારી પાડી, તયારે હું સાવચેત થઈ. એ વેલાએ મેં આસપાસ જોયું, એટલે મને જણાયું કે મારી છોકરીને સખત ઈજા થઈ હતી, તેમજ મારો હાથ કચડાયો હતો અને ગાડી પુર જોરમાં દોડતી હતી. મરનારનાં માથાં ઉપર એથી ઈજા થઈ હતી. એ વેલાએ એક બીજો ભીખારી મારી નજદીકમાં સુતો હતો. મરનારને આસપીટલમાં લઈ જવામાં આવી હતી, એ વેલાએ તેણીનાં કાનમાંથી લોહી વેહેતું હતું. બાદ તયાંજ તેણી મરણ પામી હતી. ગાડીવાલા (આરોપી) એ બાજુ થવાને કશી બુમ ન પાડી હતી. મરનારને ઈજા થઈ તે આગમજ તેણી તંદરોસત હાલતમાં હતી. મને ખબર ન હતી કે તે રસતા ઉપર ગાડી ઘોડાનો આવજાવ છે, અગરજો મને ખબર હતે તો કદી બી હું તયાં (મરનાર) મારી છોકરી સાથે સુતે નહી. એ દીવસ સોમવારનો હતો જે પછી આજ સુધી બે સોમવારો પસાર થયા છે.

આરોપીએ જણાવયું કે સાક્ષીને ઉલટપાલટ તપાસતો નથી. મારી ગાડી દરવાજામાં દાખલ થઈ તે વેલાએ મને રસતા ઉપર સુતેલું કોઈ માલમ પડયું નહી.

રૂસતમજી ફરદુનજીએ મી૰ લીટલની તપાસમાં જણાવ્યું કે હું પારસી ધરમગુરૂ છું. આરોપીને ઓલખું છું, તે મારી સાથે તેડાં કરવા ગાડી હાંકતો હતો. આરોપી ગાડી ફેરવનાર પારસીની નોકરી-માં છે. પારસી સ્ત્રીઓ સાથે લગનનાં તેડાં કરવા આરોપીની ગાડીમાં અમો જતાં હતાં. એ વેલાએ સવારનો દશ કલાકનો વખત હતો. અમો વહાડ-યાની ચાલીમાં તેડાં કરવા માટે, વહાડયાનાં આત-શબેહેરામને રસતેથી તયાં ગયાં હતાં. ડાબી બાજુ તરફના દરવાજામાં ગાડીએ વલાંણ લીધી તે વેલાએ ઘોડો ચાલતો હતો. અમો અંદર (દરવાજાની) દા-ખલ થયાં, તે વેલાએ ઘોડાવાલાએ બુમ મારી તે મેં સાંભલી. કારણ કે તે વેલાએ તેડાંનાં લીસટ ઉપર મારૂં ધયાન ખેંચાયું હતું. તેણે બુમ પાડી કે "ચાલ બાજુ." બાજુ થવાને માટે આરોપીએ ૮-૧૦ વરસની છોકરીને જણાવયું અને ગાડી ચાલુજ હતી. અમો આગલ વધયા, તયાર બાદ મને જણાયું કે કોઈના ઉપરથી ગાડી ફરી ગઈ હતી, પણ તે કોણ હતું તેની મને ખબર પડી નહી. આરોપીને મેં જણાવયું કે આગલ હાંકવા આગમજ તેં જોયું હતું કે નહી? અતરે મેં મરનારની માતાને બુમ પાડતી સાંભલી હતી. સોનાપોરની ગલી આગલ સ્ત્રીઓએ ઉતરી પડી તુરતવેલા તેડાં કરવાનું માંડીવાલયું, કારણ કે

ઉપલા બનાવથી તેમને અપસગન નડવા હતા. એ બાદ પોલીસ સીપાઈ તયાં આવયો અને આરોપીને ગાડી સાથે લઈ ગયો હતો. બાદ મરનારને કારોનરની તપાસ વેલાએ જોઈ હતી, જેમાં મેં જુબાની આપી હતી.

મી૦ લીટલે માજીસટરેટથી જાણવા માગયું કે કારોનરે આરોપીની સેશનસ કમીટ કરયો છે, તયારે તમને આરોપીને જામીન ઉપર છોડવાની સતા છે કે નહી?

માજીસટરેટ—મેં કારોનર ઉપર એ વીશે લખી જણાવયું કે આરોપીને જામીન ઉપર કાં ન છોડવો? મને જવાબ મલયો છે કે આરોપીએ એવી કશી અરજ કારોનર સનમુખ કરી ન હતી. હું તેને રૂપયા ૧૦૦ ના જામીન ઉપર છોડવાનો હુકમ કરૂં છું. આરોપીને એ હુકમ સાથે કારોનર સનમુખ મોકલવામાં આવશે અને જો તેવણ દરૂસત ધારશે તો આરોપીને છોડવાનો હુકમ કરશે. તેને એકદમ છોડવાનો હુકમ કરવાની મને સતા નથી, કારણ કે કારોનરે આરોપીને સેશનસ કમીટ કરયો છે.

ગાડી ભાડે ફેરવનાર પેસતનજી એદલજી આરોપીના જામીન થવાને કબુલ થયા હતા. એ પછી વધુ તપાસ મુલતવી રહી હતી.

PART III.

GUJARATI VOCABULARY TO THE READING LESSONS.

CONTRACTIONS.

Ar. = Arabic.
Eng. = English.
G. or Guj. = Gujarātī.
H. or Hind. = Hindī.
P. or Pers. = Persian.
Sk. or Sansk. = Sanskṛit.
U. or Urd. = Urdū.
m., *f.*, *n.* = masculine, feminine, neuter.
adj. = Adjective.
adv. = Adverb.
pr. n. = Proper name.
v. gr. = See Grammar.
postp. = Postposition.
Etc., etc., etc.

VOCABULARY.

A and Ā (અ and આ).

A, *dem. adj.*, this, these (*v.* gr.).

Abdul Fāt Lodī, *m.*, (Pers. عبد الفاتح لودي), pr. n. of a chief of Multān.

Abdul Fazl, *m.* (Pers. عبد الفضل), pr. n. of the Vazīr of King Akbar.

Abdul Khāñ, *m.* (Pers. عبد الخان), pr. n. of a Muḥammadan chief.

Abdullā, *m.* (Ar. عبد الله), pr. n. of an Arab.

Abdul Malik, *m.* (Ar. عبد الملك), pr. n. of a man.

Abdul Motāleb, *m.* (Ar. عبد المطّلب), pr. n. of an Arab, 'Abdu'l Muṭṭalib.

Abdul Rehemān, *m.* (Ar. عبد الرحمن), pr. n. of an Arab, 'Abdu'r Raḥmān.

Abhimān, *n.*, pride, arrogance.

Abrūdār, *adj.* (Pers. أبرودار), honorable.

Abū Bakar, *m.* (Ar. أبو بكر), pr. n. of an Arab, Abū Bakr.

Abūl Husen, *m.* (Ar. أبو الحسين) pr. n. of a man, Abū 'l Ḥusain.

Abū Tāleb, *m.* (Ar. أبو طالب), pr. n. of an Arab, Abū Ṭālib.

Ādam Khāñ, *m.* (Pers. أدم خان), pr. n. of a Muḥammadan chief.

Adbhut, *adj.*, wonderful, strange, marvellous.

Adekhāī, *f.*, envy, jealousy; *a.*, *karvī*, to envy.

Adhik, *adj.* and *adv.*, more.

Adhikār, *m.*, power, authority; right.

Adhipati, *m.*, Editor (of a paper); ruler, master.

Ādilśāh, *m.* (Pers. عادل شاه), pr. n. of a man.

Afgānastān, *n.* (Pers. افغانستان), Afghānistān.

Āgaḷ, *postp.*, before, in front of.

Agamaj, *adv.*, before, previously.

Agar, *conj.*, (Pers. اگر), if.

Agarjo, *conj.*, (Pers. اگر and Guj. *jo*), if.

Agatya, *f.*, importance, need: *agatya-no*, (*nī*, *-nuñ*), important.

Agiārm-o, -ī, -uñ, *num. adj.*, eleventh.

Agl-o, -ī, -uñ, *adj.*, former.

Agnī, *f.*, fire.

Āgrā, *n*, the city of Āgrā.

Ahmadnagar, *n.*, the city of Aḥmadnagar.

Āīne Akbarī (Pers. phrase آئینۂ اکبری), Mirror of Akbar.

Ajāeb, *n.* (Ar. Pl. عَجائب from عَجیب), wonders, wonderful things, miracles: *adj*, wondrous.

Ajāṇ-o, -ī, -uñ, *adj.*, ignorant, (of -*thī*).

Ajim, *m.* (Ar. عاظِم), pr. n. of a son of Aurangzeb.

Ajmer, *n.*, the city of Ajmere.

Ākār, *m.*, form, shape.

Ākāś, *n.*, the sky, heaven; the æther.

Akbar, *m.*, (Ar. اکبر), pr. n. Emperor Akbar.

Ākhare, *adv.* (Ar. آخِر and Guj. term. *e*), at last, finally.

Ākh-o, -ī, -uñ, *adj.*, the whole, all.

Ālamgīr, *m.* (Pers. عالمگیر), pr. n. and title of Aurangzeb. ('Ālamgīr = 'World-seizer.')

Alā uddīn, *m.* (Ar. علا الدّین), pr. n. of a man, 'Alā u'ddīn.

Alaukik, *adj.*, extraordinary, novel, unusual.

Alī, *m.* (Ar. علي), pr. n., 'Alī.

Al Kadr (Ar. القدر), name of the night (called in full لَيْلَةُ القدر, *i.e.* 'night of power *or* of fate'), on which the Qurân began to be revealed.

Alptagīn, *m.*, pr. n. of a chief (Turkish).

Al-siddīk, *m.* (Ar. الصِّدّيق, the truthful), pr. n. of an Arab.

Al-zobair, *m.* (Ar. الزُّبير), pr. n. of an Arab, Az-Zubair.

Ame, *p. pron.*, we (*v.* gr.).

Amaldār, *m.* (Pers. عملدار), officer, official, governor.

Amarkoṭ, *n.*, pr. n. of a town.

Amburgaḍh, *n.*, pr. n. of a town and fort.

Amīnā, *f.*, (Ar. آمنة), Āmina, pr. n. of Muḥammad's mother.

Amīr, *m.* (Ar. أمیر), a nobleman.

Amo, *p. pron.*, we (*v.* gr.).

Ānākānī, *f.*, reluctance, hesitation; *ā. karvī*, to hesitate.

Anangapāḷ, *m.*, pr. n. of a son of Jaipāl.

Aṇāvavuñ, *v. tr.*, to cause to bring; *viśvās aṇ.*, to cause to believe, cause to accept.

Andar, *postp.* (Pers. اندر), within, inside.

Āndhḷ-o, -ī, -uñ, *adj.*, blind.

Ane, *conj.*, and.

Angikār, *n.*, acceptation; *a. karvuñ*, to accept.

Āngḷī, *f.*, a finger, a toe.

Angrej, *m.* (Urdū انگریز), an Englishman.

Angrejī, *adj.*, English.

Anjāṇpaṇuñ, *n.*, ignorance, want of intention.

Ānkh, *f.*, an eye.

Antahkaraṇ, *n.*, the heart, conscience.

Anubhav, *m.*, experience.

Āṇvuñ, *v. tr.*, to bring.

Apamān, *n.*, dishonour, insult.

Apaṇn-o, -ī, -uñ, *adj. pron.*, our, ours (incl., *v.* gr.).

Apasagaṇ } *m.*, an ill omen.
Apaśakun }

Apavās, *m.*, a fast, fasting.

Apāvavuñ, *v. tr.*, to cause to give (fr. *āpvuñ*).

Apāvuñ, *v.* (pass. of *āpvuñ*), to be given.

Āpṇe, *p. pron.*, we (incl., *v.* gr.).

Āpṇ-o, -ī, -uñ, *pron. adj.*, our, ours (incl., *v.* gr.).

Āpvuñ, *v. tr.*, to give: (with *oblique infin.* of preceding verb), to permit.

Arab, *m.* (Ar. عرب), an Arab; *Arab lok*, Arabs.

Arabastān, *n.* (Pers. عربستان), Arabia.

Arabī, *adj.*, Arabian, Arabic.

Araj, *f.* (Ar. عرض), a request, representation.

Ārākān, *m.*, pr. n. of a province.

Ārambh, *m.*, beginning.

Ārop, *m.*, accusation, charge.

Āropī, *m.*, accused, defendant criminal.

Asal } *adj.* (Ar. اصل),
Asal-n-o, -ī, -uñ } original, old, ancient.

Āsare, *adv.*, about, nearly

Āścharya, *n.*, surprise, marvel; *adj.*, wonderful, strange.

Asof Khāñ, *m.*, pr. n. of a brother of Nūr Jahān.

Āspās, *postp.*, near, close to, at hand.

Aśuddh, *adj.*, impure, unclean.

Ātaś, *m.* (Pers. آتش), fire.

Ātaśbeherām, *m.*, a fire-temple.

Āṭh, *num. adj.*, eight.

Āṭhm-o, -ī, -uñ, *adj.*, eighth.

Athvā, *conj.*, or.

Ati, *adv.*, very, extremely.

Atīk, *m.* (Ar. عتيق, liberated slave), pr. n.

Aṭkāv, *m. f.*, obstruction, hindrance.

Aṭkāvavuñ, *v. tr.*, to prevent, hinder; refuse.

Ātmā, *m.*, a spirit, soul.

Atre, *adv.*, here, hither.

Aurangjeb, *m.* (Pers. اورنگزیب), pr. n., Aurangzeb.

Avāj, *m.* (Pers. Urdū آواز, *f.*) voice, sound.

Āvakār, *m.*, a courteous reception.

Avasar, *m.*, opportunity, occasion; period.

Avasthā, *f.*, state, condition.

Āvavuñ, *v. intr.*, to come.

Aviśvāsī, *adj.*, unbelieving; *subs. m.*, unbeliever.

Āvjāv, *m.*, coming and going, traffic.

Āv-o, -ī, -uñ, *adj.*, like this, such, so.

Āyarkūṭ, *m.*, pr. n. of a man.

Ayāz, *m.*, pr. n. of a man.

Ayodhyā, *m.*, Province of Oude.

B and Bh (બ and ભ).

Bachāv, *m.*, preservation, deliverance.

Bachpaṇuñ, *n.*, childhood.

Bachvuñ, *v. intr.*, to escape.

Bād, *adv.* and *postp.* (Ar. بَعْد), after, afterwards.

Badh-o, -ī, -uñ, *adj.*, all.

Bǎhādūr, *adj.*, brave, gallant; *m.*, a hero (Pers. بهادر).

Bǎhādurī, *f.*, bravery, courage (Pers. بهادری).

Bahānuñ, *n.*, excuse, pretext.

Bahār, *m.*, district of Bĕhār.

Bǎhār } Baher } *adv.*, out, outside; *b. paḍvuñ*, to issue, happen, result, turn out.

Bahu, *adj.*, many, much.

Bahvuñ, *v. intr.*, to flow, pour.

Bāiḍī, *f.*, a lady, a woman, a wife.

Bajār, *n.* (Pers. بازار), street, market, *bāzār*.

Bājū, *f.* (Pers. بازو), side; *adv.*, to one side, aside; *b. thavuñ*, to go aside, get out of the way.

Bakheḍo, *m.*, tumult, quarrel, contention.

Bākī, *f.*, the remainder (Ar. باقي); *adj.*, remaining.

Baḷ, *n.*, power, strength, might.

Bāḷak, *n.*, a child, a boy.

Baluchistān, *n.*, Balūchistān (Beloochistan).

Baḷvuñ, *v. intr.*, to be on fire, to burn, be burnt.

Bāḷvuñ, *v. tr.*, to set on fire, burn; *intens.*, *b. nāñkhvuñ*.

Banāras, *n.*, city of Benares.

Banāv, *m.*, event, accident; accord.

Banāvaṭ, *f.*, an invention.

Banāvavuñ, *v. tr.*, to do, make.

Banḍ, *n.*, rebellion, insurrection; *b. uṭhāvavuñ*, to stir up rebellion.

Bandhāvuñ, *v.* (pass. of Bāndhvuñ, *q. v.*), to be bound, to be built; *Bandhāī gaelā lohīthī*, from clotted blood.

Bandhe, *adj.*, both.

Bāndhvuñ, *v. tr.*, to tie, bind; to build, to set up.

Bandīkhānuñ, *n.* (bandī + Pers. خانه), prison.

Bandīvan, *m.*, a prisoner.

Bangāḷā, *m.*, Province of Bengal.

Banne, *adj.*, both (*also* Bandhe).

Banvuñ, *v. intr.*, to come to pass, to happen, take place; to be made, to be done.

Bāp, *m.*, father.

Bār, *num. adj.*, twelve.

Barābar, *adj.* (Pers برابر). right, exact, equal, adequate.

Bārm-o, -ī, -uñ, *num. adj.*, twelfth.

Barobar, *adj.* (*v.* barābar), equal.

Basro, pr. n. (Ar. بصرة), the city of Baṣra.

Batāvavuñ, *v. tr.*, to explain, state, show.

Bāyḍī, *f.* (*vide* Bāiḍī), a woman, wife.

Be, *adj. num.*, two; *be be*, two each, two by two.

Bedarkārī, *f.* (Pers. بیدرکاری), indifference, carelessness.

Beḍī, *f.*, a fetter, manacle.

Beḍnor, *n.*, pr. n. of a place.

Begam, *f.* (Pers. بیگم), woman's title, wife of a *beg*, princess.

Beher-o, -ī, -uñ, *adj.*, deaf.

Berām, *m.* (Pers. بهرام), pr. n. of last king of Ghaznī.

Besāḍvuñ, *v. tr.*, to cause to sit, seat, set.

Besvun, *v. intr.*, to sit down (*v. irreg. vv.*).

Beṭī, *f.*, a daughter.

Bevakuf, *adj.* (Pers. بیوقوف), senseless, silly.

Bhāḍuñ, *n.*, hire, fare, rent.

Bhāg, *m.*, part, portion, division, share.

Bhāgī, *f.*, a girl's proper name.

Bhagvāndās, *m.*, pr. n. of a king of Jaipur.

Bhāgvuñ, *v. tr.*, to break, shatter; *intens.*, *bhāgī nāñkhvuñ.*

Bhāī, *m.*, brother, cousin.

Bhakti, *f.*, prayer, adoration, worship.

Bhanḍol, *m.*, capital, stock, fund.

Bhāngvuñ, *v. tr.*, to break, shatter.

Bhaṇī, *postp.*, towards, -ward.

Bhanjghaḍ } Bhanjgaḍ } *f.*, intricacy, discussion, altercation.

Bhaṇvuñ, *v. tr.*, to learn.

Bharavaṭīo, *m.*, a beam of wood.

Bhāre, *adj.*, heavy.

Bhārmal, *m.*, pr. n. of a King of Jaipur.

Bharoso, *m.*, hope, confidence; *tene . . . b. beṭho*, he had confidence.

Bhartār } Bharthār } *m.*, a husband.

Bharvuñ, *v. tr.*, to fill.

Bhāśā, *f.*, speech, language.

Bhāśāṇ } Bhāshaṇ } *n.*, a speech, an address.

Bhāṭiā, *n.*, pr. n. of a town.

Bhatrijo, *m.*, a brother's son, nephew.

Bhay, *m.*, fear, dread; danger.

Bheṭ, *f.*, an interview.

Bheṭvuñ, *v. tr.*, to meet, to embrace.

Bhevāḍ, *n.*, pr. n. of a city.

Bhīkārī, *m.*, a beggar.

Bhīkh, *f.*, beggary, begging; *b. māgvī*, to beg.

Bhīmdev, *m.*, pr. n. of a Hindū.

Bhīmī, *f.*, pr. n. of a woman.

Bhomiyo, *m.*, a guide.

Bhul, *f.*, a blunder.

Bhulchuk, *f.*, error and omission.

Bhut, *m.*, an evil spirit, goblin, ghost.

Bī, *conj.* (Urdū بهي), also, too.

Bījāpur, *n.*, pr. n. of a town.

Bijo, -ī, -uñ, *num. adj.*, seoond, other.

Bilkul } *adv.* (Ar. بِالْكُلّ), altogether.
Bilkull }

Binā, *f.*, circumstance, event.

Bokhārā, *m.*, the district of Bukhārā (Pers. بخارا).

Bol, *m.*, a word.

Bolāvavuñ, *v. tr.*, to call, summon.

Bolvuñ, *v. tr.* and *intr.*, to speak, to say.

Brāhmaṇ, *m.*, a Brāhmaṇ.

Bum, *f.* (Pers. بانگ, often pronounced *bũng*), a noise, shout, cry; *b. mārvī* or *b. pāḍvī*, to cry out, shout.

Ch and chh (ચ and છ).

Chaḍhāī, *f.*, an ascent, assault, incursion.

Chaḍhvuñ, *v. intr.*, to ascend, mount up; *intens.*, *-javuñ*, *āvavuñ*.

Chākar, *m.*, a servant (Pers. چاکر).

Chākarī, *f.* (Pers. چاکري), service, position.

Chāl, *f.*, gait; conduct, walk.

Chālākī, *f.*, cleverness, cunning (Pers. چالاکی).

Chalāvavuñ, *v. tr.*, to cause to go, send off, fire (a gun), set going, circulate.

Chālī, *f.*, a number of houses (small) in one block (chawl).

Chāḷīs, *num. adj.*, forty.

Chaḷkāṭ, *m.*, brightness, brilliancy.

Chālu, *adj.*, in motion, moving; current.

Chālvuñ, *v. intr.*, to go, walk; to keep on, to last; to be current; *chālto mahino*, the present month.

Chamatkār, *m.*, a miracle, a wonder.

Chāmuṇḍ, *n.*, pr. n. of a city.

Chāndbībī, *f.*, pr. n. of a queen of Aḥmadnagar.

Chandr, *m.*, the moon.

Changām, *n.*, name of a place.

Charitra, *n.*, narrative, memoir.

Chaud, *num. adj.*, fourteen.

Chelo, *m.*, a disciple, follower.

Cherkulī, *n.*, pr. n. of a place.

Chetavaṇī, *f.*, a caution, a warning.

Chhān-o, -ī, -uñ, secret, private.

Chhaṭā, *f.*, style (of speaking).

Chhaṭādār, *m.*, one possessed of style.

Chhaṭhṭh-o, -ī, -uñ, *adj.*, sixth.

Chhe, *v.*, is, are (3rd sing. and pl. and 2nd sing. of √chha, *q. v.* gr.).

Chhedo, *m.*, limit, boundary, end.

Chhek, *adv.*, at length, quite.

Chhell-o, -ī, -uñ, *adj.*, the last.

Chhīnāvavuñ, *v. tr.*, to snatch away (*intens.* chh. levuñ).

Chhoḍavavuñ, *v. tr.*, to deliver, rescue.

Chhoḍvuñ, to leave, abandon, cease; *chhoḍī devuñ*, intensative.

Chhokr-o, *m.*, -ī, -uñ, a boy (girl, child), son (daughter).

Chhuñ, *v.* (1st sing. of √chha, *v.* gr.), am.

Chhuṭ-o, -ī, -uñ, *adj.*, free; *chh. mukvuñ* or *karvuñ*, to set free.

Chhuṭvuñ, *v. intr.*, to get free, be delivered, escape.

Chīchārī } *f.*, a scream, yell; *c.*
Chichiārī } *pāḍvī*, to scream.

Chīrvuñ, *v. tr.*, to tear, rip; *chīrī nāñkhvuñ*, to rip up, *intens.*

Chitoḍ, *n.*, pr. n., Chitore (town).

Chittākarshak, *adj.*, heart-attracting.

Chohāṇ, *m.*, name of a family of Rajpūt kings of Ajmere.

Chokas, *adj.*, precise, exact.

Chokasāī, *f.*, caution, care, carefulness; exactness, precision.

Choth-o, -ī, -uñ, *adj.*, fourth.

D soft and dh (ડ and ઢ).

Dādo, *m.*, a paternal grandfather.

Dago, *m.* (Ar. دغا), deceit, treachery, perfidy.

Dahāḍo }
Dāhāḍo } *m.*, a day.

Dāhīr, *m.*, pr. n., Dāhīr.

Dâkhal, *adj.*, entering (Ar. داخل); *dākhal thavuñ*, to enter; *d. karvuñ*, to cause to enter.

Dakhaṇ, *f.*, the south, the Deccan.

Dakshiṇ, *f.*, the south; the Deccan: *adj.*, southern.

Damāskas, *n.*, pr. n., the city of Damascus.

Dāniyāl, *m.*, Daniel, pr. n. of 3rd son of Emperor Akbar.

Dānt, *m.*, tooth.

Dārā, *m.*, pr. n. of one of Aurangzeb's brothers.

Darbār, *f.*, a levee, audience, (at court).

Darek, *adj.* (Pers. دریک), each, every.

Dariā, *f.*, the sea.

Dariāī, *adj.*, marine.

Dārūḍīo, *m.*, a drunkard.

Darust, *adj.* (Pers درست), correct, right.

Darvājo, *m.* (Pers. دروازه), a door, a gate; a doorway.

Das } ten; *das kalāke*, at ten
Daś } o'clock.

Dās, *m.*, a slave, a servant.

Dasm-o, -ī, uñ, tenth.

Dattak, *m.*, an adopted son.

Dāṭvuñ, to bury.

Dayā, *f.*, mercy, pity.

Dayāḷu, *adj.*, merciful.

Dekhāḍvuñ, *v. tr.*, to cause to see, to show.

Dekhāituñ, *adj. n.*, apparent, visible.

Dekhāv, *m.*, appearance, sight, a vision.

Dekhvuñ, *v. tr.*, irregular (*v.* gr.), to see, perceive.

Deheruñ } *n.*, a temple, pagoda.
Debaruñ }

Deś, *m.*, country, land.

Dev, *m.*, a deity, a god.

Devalnagar, *n.*, pr. n., old name of Karāchī.

Devavāṇī, *f.*, a divine voice, a (heathen) oracle.

Dhaṇī, *m.*, master, owner.

Dhāraṇ, *n.*, market price; holding; taking up: *d. karvuñ*, to adopt (a title), assume.

Dharm, *m.*, religion.

Dharmguru, *m.*, religious teacher, priest.

Dhāro, *m.*, law, rule; custom, manners: *dhāro paḍyo*, the law (custom) was established.

Dhārvuñ, *v. tr.*, to set, fix; to think, consider.

Dhartī, *f.*, the earth.

Dhartīkanp, *m.*, an earthquake.

Dhikkār, *m.*, disdain, scorn; hatred.

Dhīre, *adj.*, slowly.

Dhob(h)ī Talāv, name of a part of Bombay, Dhobī Talāo.

Dhyān, *n.*, attention; *d. āpvuñ* (— upar), to pay attention to.

Dīdh-o, -ī, -uñ (part. of Devuñ), *v.* gr., irregular verbs.

Dīkro, *n.*, a son.

Dīkrī, *f.*, a daughter.

Dilhī, *n.*, the city Delhi.

Din, *m.*, a day.

Diśā, *f.*, state, condition.

Dīṭh-o, -ī, -uñ, *v.* (part. of Dekhvuñ, q. v.), seen.

Dīvān-o, -ī, -uñ, *adj.* (Pers. دیوانه), mad; *dīvāno*, subs. *m.*, a madman.

Divas, *m.*, a day.

Doḍvuñ, *v. intr.*, to run.

Dolat, *f.*, wealth (Ar. دَوْلَة).

Dravya, *n.*, wealth, property.

Duhkh (દુ:ખ), *n.*, pain, suffering, distress.

Duniyāñ }
Duniyā } *f.* (Ar. دُنيا), the world, the present world.
Duniā }

Dūr, *adj.*, distant, far.

Duśman, *m.*, enemy (Pers. دُشْمَن).

Dūt, *m.*, a messenger, an angel.

Duvāī, *f.*, prayer, blessing (Ar. دعا); *d. feravavuñ*, to have prayers offered for himself in the mosques, as sign of his being emperor.

Ḍ hard and ḍh (ડ and ઢ).

Ḍāb-o, -ī, -uñ, *adj.*, left (side, hand).

Ḍhaglo, *m.*, a large heap, accumulation.

Ḍhab } *f.*, style, air, method;
Ḍhap } idiom.

Ḍhongī, *m.*, religious pretender, hypocrite.

Ḍoḷo, *m.*, eye; sight.

E (એ).

E, *demonst. adj.*, that.

-e, postp. (see gr.), in, at, by (agent.).

-e, affix, sometimes adds emphasis, as *eke*, 'even one;' 'just one:' *traṇe*, 'all three,' &c.

Ebn Hāreth, *m.*, pr. n. (Ar. ابن حارث), Ibn Ḥārith, surname of Zaid, q. v.

Ek, *num. adj.*, one; a.

Ekānt, *f.*, a private place, privacy: *ekāntno* (*nī, nuñ*), private.

Ekāntī, *adj.*, belonging to privacy, private.

Ekdam, *adv.* (ek + Pers. دم), at once, instantly.

Ekmek, *adj.*, mixed, mutual; one another.

Ekṭh-o, -ī, -uñ, *adj.*, together, collected; — *karvuñ*, to collect.

Elchī, *m.* (Turk. ایلچی), an ambassador.

Ém, *adv.*, thus, so, in this way.

Eṭle, *particle*, then, that is to say.

Eṭlo, -ī, -uñ, *adj.*, so much, thus much: *eṭlāmān*, meanwhile: *eṭle*, then; that is to say, *viz.*

Ev-o, ī, -uñ, *adj. pr.*, such as this; thus.

F (ફ or ફ઼).

Fakat, *adv.*, only, simply (Ar. فقط).

Fariād } *f.*, complaint, supplica-
Fariyād } tion, (*Pers.* فریاد).

Farīthī, *adv.*, again, once more.

Farvuñ, *v. intr.*, to turn, to move about, to travel, perambulate.

Fateh, *f.* (Ar. فتح), victory.

Fāvavuñ, *v. intr.*, to succeed; to find convenient.

Felāvavuñ, *v. tr.*, to spread, cause to spread, cause to extend.

Feravavuñ, *v. tr.*, to cause to turn, to turn; to circulate, to run a trap (for hire).

Firdosī, *m.*, pr. n. of the great

Persian Poet (author of Shāh-nāmeh).

Foj, *f.*, army (Ar. فَوْج); *Polīs foj*, police force.

G and gh (ગ and ઘ).

Gabhrāvuñ, *v. intr.*, to be confused.

Gādi, *f.*, a throne.

Gāḍi, *f.*, a carriage (of any sort).

Gaznavī } *adj.*, Ghaznavite.
Gajhnavi }

Gakhkar, *m.*, name of a mountain tribe in the north of the Panjāb.

Galī, *f.*, a lane.

Gām, *n.*, a village.

Gāmḍuñ, *n.*, a small village, hamlet.

Game, *conj.*, even if, although.

Gaṇāvuñ, *v.* (pass. of gaṇvuñ, q.v.), to be accounted.

Ganān, *n.* (corr. fr. jnān), knowledge.

Gaṇvuñ, *v. tr.*, to count, reckon.

Garhasth, *m.* (*v.* grihasth), a gentleman.

Garīb, *adj.* (Ar. غَرِيب), poor, humble.

Garvishṭ, *adj.*, proud, haughty.

Gayo, gaī, gayuñ, *v.* (past of javuñ, irreg.), *v.* gr.

Gera-upayog, *m.* (Hybrid, Ar. غَيْر + up.), uselessness.

Gervājabī, *adj.* (Ar. واجبي + غَيْر), improper.

Ghaṇīkvār, *adv.*, pretty often, several times.

Ghaṇ-o, -ī, -uñ, much, many.

Ghaṇ-o khar-o, *adj.*, very many.

Ghaṇto, *m.*, a belt.

Ghar, *n.*, a house; household.

Gharḍ-o, -ī, -uñ, *adj.*, old, aged, advanced in years.

Gharḍāvarḍāo, *m. pl.*, ancestors, forefathers.

Ghusvuñ, *v. intr.*, to push one's way in.

Gher (for ghare), in, to a house; home, at home.

Ghoḍāvāḷo, *m.*, a horsekeeper, groom, driver.

Ghoḍo, *m.*, a horse: *ghoḍe*, on a horse.

Ghor, *m.* (Pers گور, wild ass), appellation of Bahrām, king of Ghaznī.

Ghorī, *adj.*, belonging to, descendant from Bahrām Ghor.

Ghuṭaṇ, *m.* } a knee: *ghuṭṇīe paḍvuñ*, to fall on one's knees, to kneel down.
Ghuṭṇī, *f.* }

Gijhnī, the city of (غَزْني) Ghaznī.

Govaḷkonṭā, *n.*, name of a fortress in the Deccan.

Gufā, *f.*, a cave.

Grihasth, *m.*, a gentleman.

Gujarāt, *n.*, name of a city and province.

Gujārvuñ, *v. tr.*, to cause to pass, to cause to come upon.

Gulâm, *m.* (Ar. غلام), a male slave.

Gulāmḍī, *f.*, *dim.*, a female slave.

Guṇ, *m.*, qualities, attributes, virtues.

Gusse, *adj.* (Hind. غصّے from Ar. غصّة), angry.

Gvāliyar, *n.*, the city of Gwalior.

H (ह).

Habsī } *adj.*, negro (Ar. حبشي).
Habśī }

Haidrābād, *n.*, city of Ḥaidarābād.

Hājar, *adj.* (Ar. حاضر), present, in attendance.

Hajār, *num.*, a thousand (P. هزار).

Hajrat, *m.* (Ar. حضرة), word used to show respect among Muhammadans, as *S'ri* among Hindūs, His Highness, Saint.

Hākem, *m.* (Ar. حاكم), ruler, governor.

Hāl, *adv.* (Ar. حال, state), at present, now.

Hālat, *f.*, state, condition (Ar. حالة).

Haḷve, *adv.* (often *doubled*), gently, gradually, slowly.

Hame, *pron.*, we, *v.* gr. (*ame* is the better form in Guj.).

Hamṇāñ, *adv.*, now, at present.

Hānī } *f.*, loss, injury, damage.
Hāṇī }

Hāñkvuñ, *v. tr.*, to drive, urge; H. *kāḍhvuñ*, expel.

Hāñsal (corr. from Ar. حاصل) karvuñ, *v. tr.*, to gain, acquire, attain to.

Hār, *f.*, a defeat; *h. khāvī*, to be defeated.

Harakat, *f.* (Ar. حَرَكة), hindrance, difficulty.

Harakh, *m.*, joy, rapture.

Harāvavuñ, *v. tr.*, to defeat.

Harīf, *m.* (Ar. حريف), rival.

Hārvuñ, *v. intr.*, to be defeated.

Haśe, *v.*, 3rd sing. fut. of *hovuñ*, to be, *v.* gr.

Hāśim } *m.*, proper name of an
Hāśem } Arab, *Hāshim*.

Hasvuñ, *v. intr.*, to laugh.

Hāth, *m.*, hand; authority.

Haṭh, *f.*, obstinacy.

Hat-o, -ī, -uñ, *v. intr.*, was (from *hovuñ*, q. v.).

Hāthī, *m.*, an elephant.

Have, *adv.*, now, at this time.

Hemu, *m.*, pr. n. of a *wazīr*.

Himat, *f.* (Ar. همّة), boldness; courage. *Himat bharelo vichār*, a bold thought.

Hindu, *m.*, a Hindū.

Hindustān, *n.*, pr. n., India, Upper India.

Hīrā, pr. n. (Ar. حراء) of a cave near Mecca.

Hisāb, *m.* (Ar. حساب), account, reckoning.

Hokins, *m.*, Captain Hawkins.

Holvavuñ, *v. tr.*, to extinguish, put out.

Holvāvuñ, *v. pass.*, to be extinguished: *h. javuñ* (intens.).

Hot (see *hovuñ* and gr. s. v.).

Hot-o, -ī, uñ, *v. intr.*, was (form of *hato* sometimes used after neg. *na*, *v.* gr.).

Hovuñ, *v. intr. aux.*, to be, to become, *v.* gr.

Humāyuñ, *m.*, pr. n. of an emperor, father of Akbar.

Hukūmat, *f.* (Ar. حكومة), rule.

Hukm, *m.* (Ar. حُكْم), command, order.

Humlo, *m.* (Ar. حمله), an attack, assault.

Huñ, *pers. pr.*, I (*v.* gr.).

Hunnar, *m.* (Pers. هنر), an art, skill.

I, and Ī (ઇ and ઈ).

Ichchhā, *f.*, a wish, desire.

Ijā, *f.*, injury, trouble (Ar. ايذا).

Ijan, *n.* (Ar. اذْن), an invitation.

Imān, *n.* (Ar. ايمان), faith, belief.

Imārat, *f.* (Ar. عمارة), a building.

Inglānḍ, *n.*, pr. n., England.

Insāfī, *adj.* (from Ar. انْصاف), just.

Irān, *m.*, pr. n., Irān, Persia.

Irānī, *adj.*, Persian.

Isā, *m.*, pr. n., Jesus (Ar. عيسي).

Isavī, *adj.* (عيسوى), Christian: *Īsavī san* (or ઈ. સ.), Christian Year, = A.D.

Īśu, *m.*, pr. n., Jesus (Ar. يسوع).

Īśvar, *m.*, God.

Īśvarī, *adj.*, divine.

J and Jh (જ and ઝ).

J, affix, adding emphasis, equivalent to *indeed* or to *italicisation*.

Jabrīyel, *m.*, pr. n. (Ar. جبريل), the angel Gabriel.

Jabr-o, -i, -uñ, *adj.* (Ar. جَبْر), mighty, powerful, great.

Jādu, *n.*, sorcery, witchcraft, magic.

Jādūgar, *m.*, sorcerer, magician (Pers. جادوگر).

Jagā, Jago, Jagyā } *f.*, (Old Pers. poet جايگاه, Urdū جگه), a place.

Jahānkhāñ, *m.*, pr. n. of a man.

Jahāñsūz, *m.* (Pers. جهانسوز), appellation of 'Alā 'uddīn Ghorī.

Jajīāvero, *m.* (Ar. جِزْية + Guj. *vero*, a tax), the *Jazia*-tax.

Jalāluddīn, *m.*, pr. n. of Akbar (Ar. جلال الدين).

Jamābandī, *f.*, revenue, land-assessment.

Jamāi, *m.*, son-in-law.

Jamīn, *f.* (Pers. زمين), land, ground.

Jāmin, *m.* (Ar. ضامن), a baillor, guaranteer, one who gives bail or security for.

Jamnā, *f.*, name of river, Jamnā.

Jamṇ-o, -ī, -uñ, *adj.*, right (of the hand).

Jān, *m.* (Pers. جان), life; *j. levo*, to slay.

Jaṇ, *m.* and *n.*, person.

Jāñhāñgīr, *m.* (Pers. جهانگیر), name of Salīm, eldest son of Akbar, Emperor Jehāñgīr.

Janam } *n.*, birth; *janm dharvuñ*,
Janm } being born.

Janm charitra, *n.*, biography.

Janmvuñ, *v. intr.*, to be born.

Janānkhānuñ, *n.* (Pers. زنانخانه), seraglio, zenana.

Jaṇāvavuñ, *v. tr.*, to cause to know, state, inform.

Jaṇāvuñ, *v.* (pass. of jāṇvuñ, q.v.), to be known.

Jāṇvuñ, *v. tr.*, to know.

Jarā, *adj.* and *adv.* (Ar. ذرّه), a little, some, (with neg.), at all.

Jārī, *adj.* (Ar. جاري), flowing, current; *jārī rākhvuñ*, to support (a custom, &c.).

Jasvantsinh, *m.*, pr. n. of a general and king of Jodhpur.

Jāt, *f.*, a tribe; caste; kind, sort.

Jātī, *f.*, gender; *adj.*, natural.

Javāb, *m.*, an answer, reply (Ar. جَوَاب).

Javāher } *n.* (corr. of Ar. pl.
Javāhir } جَوَاهِر), a jewel.

Javānī, *f.*, youth.

Javuñ, *v. intr.*, irreg. (v. gr.), to go.

Jayā (gerund. from javuñ, *v.* gr. irreg. verbs), *jayā karto*, used to go.

Jaychand, *m.*, Prince of Kanoj.

Jaypāḷ, *m.*, pr. n., Jaipāl, name of two kings of Lahore.

Jazīrat-ul-Arab (Ar. جَزِيرَةُ الْعَرَب), the Arabian Peninsula.

Je, *rel. pr.*, who, which, that; *je kaiñ*, whatever, whatsoever.

Jems, *m.*, pr. n., James (I. of England).

Jepur, *n.*, town of Jaipur (Jeypore).

Jev-o, -ī, uñ, *adj.*, such.

Jhāḍ, *n.*, a tree, a plant.

Jhājh-o, -ī, -uñ, *adj.*, much, very, more.

Jherī, *adj.* (Urdū زَهرِي), poisonous.

Jhurābandh, *adj.*, mortifying, sorrowful, sad.

Jindagī, *f.* (corr. from Pers. زِنْدَگِي), life, period of life.

Jīt, *f.*, a victory.

Jītnār, *m.*, conqueror, victor.

Jītvuñ, *v. tr.*, to overcome, conquer; *jītī levuñ*, to capture (a city).

Jīvavuñ, *v. intr.*, to live, remain alive.

Jnān, *n.*, knowledge.

Jo, *conj.*, if; *jo ke*, although.

Joḍe, *postp.*, with.

Jodhpur, *n.*, town of Jodhpore.

Joïe, *v. defect.* (*v.* gr.), it is necessary, must.

Jor, *n.* (Pers. زور), strength, power, violence.

Jovuñ, *v. tr.* (*v.* gr.), to see, behold.

Jubānī (Pers. زبان), oral evidence, speech, word of mouth.

Jud-o, -ī, -uñ, *adj.* (Pers. جدا), separate, different.

Julam, *m.* (Ar. ظلم), tyranny, cruelty.

Jun-o, -ī, -uñ, *adj*, old, ancient.

Jusrī } *f.*, yoke, sway.
Jhusrī }

Juṭhāpaṇuñ and Juṭhāṇuñ, *n.*, a lie, a fabrication.

Jūṭh-o, -ī, -uñ, false.

Jūṭhuñ, *n.*, a lie.

Jyāñ, *adv.*, where.

Jyāre, *adv.*, when.

K and Kh (ક and ખ).

Kābul, *n.*, pr. n. of a city of Afghānistān.

Kabūl, *adj.* (Ar. قبول), accepted; *k. karvuñ*, to accept, receive; agree (to do).

Kachaḍvuñ, *v. tr.*, to crush, to tread down, trample, run over; *k. nāñkhvuñ*, intens.

Kachḍāvuñ, *v.* (pass. of *kachaḍvuñ*), to be crushed.

Kāḍhvuñ, *v. tr.*, to take out, drive out, extract, draw out; *kāḍhī mukvuñ*, to drive out, *intens.*; *vakht kāḍhvuñ*, to spend time.

Kadī, *adv.* (with neg.), never; *kadī kadī*, sometimes, at times.

Kādījā, *f.* (Ar. خديجة), pr. n., Khadīja, Muḥammad's first wife.

Kaḍko, *m.*, a piece, bit, fragment.

Kāfalo, *m.* (Ar. قافلة), a caravan; *dariyāno k.*, a fleet.

Kāfar, *m.* (Ar. كافر), an unbeliever.

Kāgaḷ, *m.*, paper, a letter (Pers. كاغذ).

Kāhāḍvuñ, *v.tr.* to take out (=kāḍhvuñ, *q. v.*).

Kāhāṇī, *f.*, a story, fable, tale.

Kāiñ } *n. pron.* (*v.* gr.), some, something, any.
Kaiñ }

Kajio, *m.* (Ar. قضية), a quarrel, a lawsuit.

Kajvā, *n.*, pr. n. of a town about thirty miles from Allahābād.

Kakḍo, *m.*, a piece, bit.

Kāko, *m.*, a paternal uncle.

Kāḷ, *m.*, time, period; *teno kāḷ thayo*, his time was up, he died.

Kalāk, *f.* (Eng. clock), an hour; *das kalāke*, at ten o'clock.

Kalam, *f.* (Ar. قلم) a reed-pen, a pen.

Kālikaṭ, *m.*, town of Calicut.

Kalinjar, *n.*, city of Kalinjar.

Kalpanā, *f.*, fancy, imagination.

Kām, *n.*, work, deed.

Kāmbaksh, *m.* (Pers. کامبخش), pr. n. Kāmbakhsh, a son of Aurangzeb.

Kampanī, *f.*, the (East India) Company (Eng.).

Kāñ, *adv.*, why, wherefore?

Kān, *n.*, the ear.

Kandahār, *n.*, city of Candahār.

Kanoj, *n.*, Kanoj (Canodge).

Kanyā, *f.*, a maiden, a princess.

Kanyā Kumāri, *n.*, pr. n., Cape Comorin.

Kāpaḍ, *n.*, cloth.

Kāpvuñ, *v. tr.*, to cut; *intens.*, *kāpī nāñkhvuñ*, to cut off, cut down.

Kar, *m.*, tax; usage.

Kāraṇ, *n.*, cause, reason; *kāraṇ ke*, because.

Karāñchī, *n.*, city of Karāchī (Kurrachee).

Karāvuñ, *v.* (*pass.* of *karvuñ*), to be done.

Kārbhārī, *m.*, manager, officer.

Karīne, *v.* (*connective part.* of *karvuñ*); *postp.*, on account of; by means of, *v. gr.*

Karnal, *m.*, (Eng.) colonel.

Karnal Smith, Col. Smith.

Karnal Belī, Col. Bailey.

Karnāṭak, *m.*, the Carnatic.

Karoḍ, *num. adj.*, a *crore*, ten millions.

Kartāñ } *postp.* (orig. *part.* of *kar-*
Karttāñ } *vuñ*), than (used in comparison).

Karvuñ, *v. irreg. tr.* (*v.* gr.), to do, to make.

Kāśī, *n.*, the city of Banāras (Benares).

Kaśī, *adj. pron.* (Pārsī Guj., from Urdū کسی) any.

Kāsim, *m.*, (Ar. قاسم), pr. n., Qāsim, of a man.

Kaśmīr, *m.*, the country of Kashmīr (Cashmere).

Kathā, *f.*, a tale, story, narrative.

Kaṭko, *m.*, a piece, bit, portion.

Kaṭṭo, ī, -uñ, *adj.*, bitter, fierce, mortal (enemy).

Kavī, *m.*, a poet.

Ke, *conj.*, that; or.

Ked, *m.*, (Ar. قید), imprisonment; *k. karvuñ*, to imprison.

Kehen, *f.* and *m.*, a message.

Kehenāro, *m.*, a relator, narrator.

Kehevāvuñ, *v.* (*pass.* of *kehevuñ*), to be called; to be said, to be told.

Kehevuñ, *v. tr. irreg.* (*v.* gr.), to say, speak.

Kem, *adv.*, how? in what way?

Keptan, *m.*, (Eng.) Captain.

Kethe, *adv.*, anywhere; whence?

Keṭl-o, -ī, -uñ, *adj.*, how much? how many? *keṭlāek* or *keṭlāk*, *m.*, a good many, some considerable number (or length) of.

Kev-o, -ī, -uñ, *adj.*, what sort of?

Khabar, *f.*, news, information, tidings.

Khabardār, *adj.* (Pers. خبردار), careful, on one's guard.

Khabardārī, *f.* (Pers. خبرداري), care, carefulness.

Khachīt, *adv.*, sure, certain; *adv.*, certainly.

Khadījā, *f.* (*vide* Kādijā).

Khalī, *adj.* (Ar. خالي), empty.

Khalīfo, *m.* (Ar. خليفة), a Khalīf (Caliph).

Khālsā, *m.*, state land, government land;—*k. karvuñ*, to confiscate to the state.

Khamvuñ, *v. tr.*, to suffer, endure.

Khāñ, *m.* (Pers. خان), master, lord.

Khanagī, *adj.* (from Pers. خانه), private.

Khanḍaṇī, *f.*, tribute, fine.

Khānzamān, *m.* (Pers. خان زمان), pr. n. of a Muhammadan chief.

Kharāb, *adj.* (Ar. خراب), bad, evil; *adv.*, ill.

Kharekharuñ, *adv.*, truly, assuredly.

Kharekhāt, *adv.*, assuredly.

Khar-o, -ī, -un, *adj.*, true real, good.

Khatāb, *m.* (Ar. خطاب), title, appellation.

Khātuñ, *n.*, account, department, province.

Khavāḍuñ, *v. tr.*, to cause to eat; *hār kh.*, to inflict a defeat.

Khāvuñ, *v. tr. irreg.* (*v.* gr.), to eat; to suffer.

Khenchāvuñ, *v.* (*pass*, of *khenchvuñ*), to be pulled, dragged, etc.

Khenchvuñ, *v. tr.*, to pluck, pull, drag; *khenchī kāḍhvuñ*, *v. intens.*, to pluck out.

Khorāk, *f.* (Pers. خوراك), food.

Khorāsān, *m.*, the country of Khurāsān.

Khoṭ-o, -ī, -uñ, *adj.*, false, untrue.

Khovuñ, *v. tr.*, to lose, destroy.

Khubsūrat, *adj.* (Pers. خوبصورت), beautiful.

Khubsūratī, *f.* (Pers. خوبصورتي), beauty.

Khull-o, -ī, -un, *adj.*, open, free, plain, clear.

Khun, *n.* (Pers. خون), murder; *koīnuñ k. karvuñ*, to murder any one.

Khuṇo, *m.*, a corner, angle.

Khuś, *adj.* (Pers. خوش), pleased.

Khuśī, *f.* (Pers. خوشي), pleasure.

Khusrū, *m.* (Pers. خوسرو), Khusrau, pr. n. of a son of Bahrām.

Khusrū Malek, *m.* (Pers. خوسروملك), Khusrau Malik, grandson of Bahrām.

Kīdh-o, -ī, -uñ, a part of Karvuñ (*v. gr. irr. vv.*).

Killo, *m.* (Ar. قلعة), fort castle, fortified town.

Kīmatī, *adj.* (Pers. قیمتی), valuable.

Kināro, *m.* (Pers. کنارہ), shore, coast.

Kitāb, *f.* (Ar. کتاب), a book.

Koī, *p. pron.*, some one, any one.

Koṇ, *interr. pron.* (*v.* gr.), who?

Koṇ, *m.*, a corner, angle.

Koreś } *m.* (Ar. قریش), the Arabian
Koresh } tribe of the Quraish, to which Muḥammad belonged.

Kūch, *f.* (Pers. کوچ), a march; *k. karvī*, to march.

Kuḷ, *n*, a family, tribe, race.

Kumārpāḷ, *m.* pr. n. of a king of Gujarāt.

Kuñvar, *m.*, a prince, a youth.

Kuñvar Rāy, *m.*, pr. n. of a king of Kanoj.

Kurān, *n.* (Ar. قرآن), the Qur'ān (Coran).

Kuśal, *adj.*, happy, healthy, safe; clever.

Kutubuddīn, *m.* (Ar. قطب الدین), pr. n. of a man, Quṭb'ddīn.

Kutumb, *m.*, a family.

L (લ).

Lābh, *m.*, profit, gain, advantage.

Laḍvaiyo, *m.*, a fighter, warrior, soldier.

Laḍvuñ, *v. intr.*, to fight, battle.

Lāek, *adj.* (Ar. لائق), worthy.

Lagan, *n. pl*, marriage, wedding; *l. karvāñ*, to marry (— *sāthe*).

Lagbhag, *adv.*, nearly, almost.

Lagī, *postp.*, up to, until, till.

Lāgo, *part.* for *Lāgyo*, from *Lāgvuñ*, q. v.; *also*, imperat., 2nd pl. of *do.*

Lāgvuñ, *v. intr.*, to feel, to be produced (fruit), to begin, to attach to.

Lāhor, *n.*, the city of Lahore.

Laīne, *v.*, conn. part of *levuñ*, q. v. (see gr.).

Lākh, *adj. num.*, one hundred thousand.

Lakhāvavuñ, *v. tr.*, to cause to write, to dictate.

Lakhnāro, *m.*, (from *lakhvuñ*, *q. v.*), a writer, author.

Lakhvuñ, *v. tr.*, to write, compose.

Lāmb-o, -ī, -uñ, *adj.*, long.

Lāñch, *f.*, a bribe; *l. khāvī*, to take a bribe; *l. khavāḍvī*, to bribe.

Lās, *f.*, corpse (Pers. لعش, Ar. نعش, Urdū لاش).

Laśkar, *n.*, army (Pers. لشکر).

Lāvavuñ, *v. tr.*, to bring.

Lāyakī, *f.* (from Ar. لائق), worth, worthiness.

Levuñ, *v. tr. irreg.* (*v.* gr.), to take; *laī javuñ*, to take away, go off taking; *laī āvavuñ*, to bring.

Līdhe, *postp.*, for the sake of, on account of.

Līdh-o, -ī, -uñ, *v.* (part. of *levuñ*), *irr.*, *v.* gr.

Lohī, *n.*, blood.

Lok, *m.* and *n.*, people, a nation.

Lūchchāī, *f.*, knavery, dissolute conduct.

Lūṭ, *f.*, booty, plunder.

Lūṭvuñ, *v. tr.*, to plunder.

M (મ)

Mā, *f.*, mother.

Madad, *f.* (Ar. مَدَد), help, aid, assistance; *koīnī madad karvī*, or *koīne madad āpvī*, to aid any one.

Mādhava Rāv, *m.*, pr. n. of a man.

Madīnā, *n.* (Ar. مَدِينَة), the city of Medina.

Madrās, *n.*, the city of Madras.

Māgvuñ, *v. tr.*, to ask, beg; desire, wish.

Mahamad, *n.* (Ar. مُحَمَّد), Muḥammad; *also used in Gujarātī for* مَحْمُود, Maḥmūd of Ghaznī. (A common man's name among Muslims.)

Mahān, *adj.*, great; large.

Mahino, *m.*, a month.

Majlis, *f.* (Ar. مَجْلِس), an assembly.

Makkā, *n.*, (Ar. مَكَّة), city of Mecca.

Makkāvāḷo, *m.*, an inhabitant of Mecca.

Māl, *m.* (Ar. مال), property, goods.

Māldev, *m.*, pr. n. of a man.

Malik Ambar, *m.*, pr. n. of a *wazīr*.

Mālmatā, *f.*, Ar. مال متاع), property, possessions.

Maḷtīo, *m.*, an associate, an ally.

Mālūm, *adj.* (Ar. مَعْلُوم), known; *m. paḍvuñ*, to become known.

Maḷvuñ, *v. intr.*, to meet, come to, be obtainable.

Mamāvo, *m.*, maternal grandfather.

Man, *n.*, heart, mind.

Mān, *n.*, respect, regard, honour.

Māñ, *postp.*, in, into; *māñthī*, from among.

Manāro, *m.* (Ar. pl. مَنار from مَنارَة), a minaret, tower, turret.

Māṇas, *n.* (occasionally *m.*), a person, human being, a man.

Manāvuñ, *v.* (pass. of *mānvuñ*, q. v.), to be honoured.

Mānd-o, -ī, -uñ, *adj.* (Pers. ماندهٔ), sick.

Mandvāḍ, *m.*, sickness (hybrid word, Pers. ماندهٔ + Guj. term. *-vāḍ*).

Mānḍvuñ, *v. intr.*, to begin, commence.

Mane (from *man*, q. v.), in mind.

Mane, *pron. pers.* (from *huñ*, q. v.), me, to me.

Māñgvuñ, *v.tr.* (=*māgvuñ* q. v.), to ask, beg, desire.

Māñhe, *postp.* and *adv.*, within, among.

Māñhomañhe, *adv.*, mutually, among themselves.

Manmant-o, ī, -uñ, *adj.*, agreeable, congenial, enough.

Mānnāro, *m.*, (from *mānvuñ*, *q. v.*), one who respects.

Mānpatar, *n.*, an address of honour.

Māñs, *n.*, meat, flesh.

Mānsing, *m.*, pr. n. of a prince.

Mānvuñ, *v. tr.*, to honour, respect, observe; confess, acknowledge.

Mār, *f.*, a beating; *mār khāvī*, *f.*, to be beaten.

Maraṇ, *n.*, death; *maraṇ pāmvuñ*, to die.

Mareṭho, *n.*, Marāṭhā; *adj.* (-o, -ī, -uñ), belonging to the Marāṭhās.

Marjī, *f.*, (Ar. Pers. Urdū مَرْضِي), desire, will, pleasure.

Mār-o, -ī, -uñ, *pron. poss.*, my, mine.

Marnār, *m.f.n.*, (*agent* of *marvuñ*, q. v.), deceased.

Mārvāḍ, *m.*, the district of Mārvāḍ (Mārvāṛ).

Mārvuñ, *v. tr.*, to strike, slay; *mārī nānkhvuñ*, to kill; *mārī nañkvuñ*, to be struck dead, killed; *māryo javuñ*, to be killed.

Mās, *m.*, a month.

Māsī, *f.*, mother's sister, maternal aunt.

Māsīāī, *adj.*, belonging to one's maternal aunt.

Mastān, *adj.*, wild, excited, mad, ungovernable.

Masūd, *m.*, pr. n. (Ar. مَسْعُود), Mas'ūd.

Mat, *n.*, opinion, doctrine, dogma.

Mātā, *f.*, mother.

Māṭe, *postp.*, and *conj.*, on account of, because of; *e māṭe* or *māṭe*, therefore.

Māṭh-o, -ī, -uñ, *adj.*, bad, evil, wicked, wrong.

Māthuñ, *n.*, head, top.

Mathurā, *n.*, name of a city, Mathurā, on the Jamnā, eighty miles from Âgra.

Matlab, *m.* (Ar. مَطْلَب), purpose, object, aim.

Mātr, *adv.*, merely, only.

Medān, *n.* (Per. مَيدان), a plain, field of battle.

Mehel, *m.* (Ar. مَحَلّ), a palace (*v.* mohol).

Mehelvuñ (also *melvuñ*), to put, to keep, to leave.

Meherbānī, *f.* (Pers. مِهْرباني), kindness, favour.

Mehesūl, *f.* (Ar. مَحْصُول), ax, revenue.

Meḷvavuñ, *v. tr.*, to get, gain acquire: to mix.

Molvuñ, *v. tr.* (*-mehelvuñ*), to put, to leave, to keep.

Meñ, *pron. pers.* (*agential* of *huñ*, *v.* gr.), by me.

Mhaisūr, *n*, the town of Mysore.

Mī. (contr. for Eng. *Mister*), Mr.

Mirjā Khāñ, *m.* (Pers. ميرزا خان), pr. n. of a man, Mīrzā Khān.

Mirjumalā, *m.*, pr. n. of a man.

Misar, *m.* (Ar. مِصْر), Egypt.

Mīṭhās, *f.*, sweetness, eloquence.

Mitr, *m.*, a friend.

Moājim, *m.* (Ar. مُعاظِم), Mu'āzim, pr. n. of a son of Aurangzeb.

Mogal, *m.* (Pers. مُغُل), a Mughul (Mogul).

Moh, *n.*, facination, charm.

Mohābat Khāñ, *m.* (Pers. مُحَبَّت خان), Muḥabbat Khān, pr. n. of a noble.

Mohol, *m.*, a palace (Ar. مَحَلّ), = *mehel.*

Mokalāvavuñ, *v. tr.*, to cause to send.

Mokalelāpaṇuñ, *n.*, the character or office of one sent; apostleship.

Mokalelo (*part.* of *mokalvuñ*, q. v.), one sent, an apostle, messenger.

Mokalvuñ, *v. tr.*, to send.

Mokrib Khāñ, *m.* (Per. مُقْرِب خان), Muqrib Khāñ, pr. n. of a man.

Morād, *m.* (Ar. مُراد), Murād, pr. n. of a son of Akbar.

Moṭ-o, -ī, -uñ, *adj.*, great; large, big.

Mubārak Khāñ, *m.* (Pers. مُبارَك خان), pr. n. of an Afghān.

Muddat, *f.* (Ar. مُدَّة), period of time.

Muel-o, -ī, -uñ (*part.* of *marvuñ*, q. v.), dead.

Mug-o, -ī, -uñ, *adj.*, dumb.

Mujab, *postp.* (Ar. مُوجِب), according to.

Mukadamo, *m.* (Ar. مُقَدَّمة), business, lawsuit.

Mukāvuñ, *v.*, (*pass.* of *mukvuñ*, q. v.), to be put.

Mukhī } *adj.*, chief, principal.
Mukhya }

Mukvuñ, *v. tr.*, to part; to give up, let go, release (also used as aux. v., *vide* gr.).

Mŭlak, *n.* (Ar. مُلْك), a country.

Mulākāt, *f.* (Ar. مُلاقات), an interview, meeting.

Multān, *n.*, pr. n. of a town in the Panjāb.

Multavī, *adj.* (Ar. مُلْتَوِى), delayed, adjourned.

Mumbaī, *n.*, the city of Bombay.

Mumtājmahāl, *f.*, pr. n. of a queen of Shāhjahān.

Mu-o, -ī, -uñ (*part.* of *marvuñ*, q. v.), dead.

Murād, *m.* (Ar. مُراد), pr. n. of a brother of Aurangzeb.

Murtī, *f.*, an image, idol, form.

Murtīpūjak, *adj.*, idolatrous; *m.*, an idol-worshipper.

Mūsā, *m.* (Ar. مُوسىٰ), pr. n., Moses.

Musalmān, *m.*, a Muslim, Musalmān (Pers. مُسَلمان, corr. from مُسْلمان, Pers. *pl.* of مُسْلِم).

Musalmānī, *adj.*, Muḥammadan.

Muśkelī, *f.* (from Ar. مُشْكِل), difficulty.

N (ન).

Na, *adv.*, not.

Nā, *adv.*, no; 2. *noun. f.*, refusal; *nā kahevī* (*pāḍvī*), to refuse.

Nabḷ-o, -ī, -uñ, *adj.*, weak, infirm, powerless.

Nadī, *f.*, a river.

Naḍvuñ, *v. tr.*, to obstruct, hinder.

Nagar, *n.*, city.

Nagarkoṭ, *n.*, pr. n. of city, Nagarkoṭ.

Nāhān-o, -ī, -uñ (better written *nāno*, &c.), little, small, young.

Nāhāsvuñ / Nāsvuñ } *v. intr.*, to flee, escape; *n. javuñ* (*intens.*).

Nahi / Nahīñ } *adv.*, not, no (*v. gr.*).

Nairutya, *adj.*, south-western.

Najdīk, *postp.*, near, close (Pers. نزديك).

Nām, *n.*, a name; a noun; *nāme*, by name.

Nām-no, -ī, -nñ, famous.

Nāmdār, *adj.*, famous, renowned.

Namuno, *m.*, example, specimen.

Nandrāj, pr. n. of a man.

Nā(ñ)khvuñ, *v. tr.*, to throw, toss (*used also* as an aux. to strengthen meaning).

Nañkhāvavuñ, *v. tr.*, to cause to throw.

Nañkhāvuñ, *v.* (pass. of *nāñkhvun*), to be thrown; *mārī nañkhāvuñ*, to be killed.

Nāpāk, *adj.* (Per. ناپاك), impure, unclean, defiled.

Narak, *n.*, Hell (one of the Hindū hells originally).

Nārāyaṇ Kevārī, *m.*, a Hindū (man's) name.

Narmāś, *f.* (Pers. نَرم soft), softness, gentleness.

Nāroḷ, *n.*, pr. n. of village at the S. W. corner of Delhi.

Nāś, *m.*, destruction; *v. tr.*, *nāś karvo*, to destroy.

Nas, *f.*, vein, artery.

Nathī, *adv.* (used for neg. of *chhe*, *v.* gr.), is not, are not.

Navāī, *f.*, novelty, rarity.

Navamo, -ī, -uñ, *num. adj.*, ninth.

Nav-o, -ī, uñ, *adj.*, new.

Ne (contr. from *ane*), *conj.*, and.

Ne, *postp.*, to, for (sign of *acc.*).

Nīche, *adv.* and *postp.*, below, under, down.

Nikaḷvuñ, *v. intr.*, to go out.

Nimvuñ, *v. tr.*, to appoint, nominate.

Pehelāñ, *postp.*, before (of time).

Pehel-o, -ī, -uñ, *adj.*, first.

Pehelvehel-o, -ī, -uñ } *adj.*, very
Pehelvel-o, -ī, -uñ } first, first of all.

Peśāvar, *n.*, the city of Peshāwar.

Pestanjī Edaljī, *m.*, pr. n. of a Pārsī.

Peśvo, *m.* (Pers. پیشوا title of the ruler of the Marāṭhās, Peshwā.

Peṭ, *n.*, belly, abdomen.

Pīḍ } *f.*, pain, anguish, distress,
Pīḍā } trouble.

Pitā, *m.*, father.

Pohonchvuñ, *v. intr.*, to arrive.

Pokār, *m.*, exclamation, shout.

Polilor, *n.*, name of a place.

Porṭo Novo, *n.*, name of a place, Porto Novo.

Potān-o, -ī, -uñ (from *pote*, *v.* gr.), his own, her own, &c.

Pote, *refl. pron.*, himself, herself, &c.

Prabhū, *m.*, a lord, master.

Prāchīn, *adj.*, ancient, former.

Pradhān, *m.*, minister, councillor.

Pragaṭ, *adj.*, clear, evident.

Pragaṭpaṇuñ, *n.*, revelation, manifestation.

Prajā, *f.*, progeny, descendants; subjects, a nation.

Prakaraṇ, *n.*, a topic, subject; a section.

Prakāś, *m.*, brightness, lustre, splendour.

Prakhyāt, *adj.*, famous, renowned.

Pramāṇe, *postp.*, according to.

Prāṇī, *n.*, living creature, animate being.

Prānt, *m.*, a province.

Prasār, *m.*, spread, diffusion; *p. karvo*, to spread.

Pravās, *m.*, travel, travelling, journeying.

Prithivī, *f.*, the earth.

Prithurāj, *m.*, pr. n. of a man.

Puchhvuñ, *v. tr.* (with *acc.*), to ask, enquire, question.

Pūr, *adj.*, full, perfect.

Purush, *m.*, a male, a man.

Pūrvādhikārī, *m.* (*pūrva*, before; *adhikārī*, heir, owner), former official, predecessor.

Pūrvuñ, *v. tr.*, to bury, inter.

Pushkaḷ, *adj.*, many.

Pustak, *n.*, a book, a volume.

Puṭhe, *postp.*, behind, after, in pursuit of.

Putr, *m.*, a son.

R (ર).

Rācharchīluñ, *n.*, household furniture.

Raḍvuñ, *v. intr.*, to weep, cry.

Rahevuñ, *v. intr.* (v. *rehevuñ*).

Raiyat, *f.* (Ar. رعيّة), subjects (of king): a peasant.

Rāj, *n.*, a kingdom, a reign; *rāj karvuñ*, to reign.

Sām-o, -ī, -uñ, *adj.*, opposed, hostile, against.

Samp, *m.*, unanimity, union, league.

Samrāvavuñ, *v. tr.*, to cause to adorn, cause to repair.

San, *m.* (Ar. سَنَة), year (Christian calendar); age, epoch (Chr.).

Sandhe, *adv.*, everywhere.

Sandhī, *f.*, union, junction; opportunity.

Sang, *postp.*, together with.

Sang, *m.*, pr. n. of a King of Udaipur.

Sānje = sānjhre, q. v.

Sānjh, *f.*, evening.

Sāñjhre, *adv.*, in the evening.

Sāñkaḷ, *f.*, a chain.

Sanmukh, *postp.*, in presence of, before.

Santān, *m.* and *n.*, progeny, descendants.

S'ānti, *f.*, comfort, rest, peace of mind.

Sar, *postp.*, on, upon, on account of.

Sar, *m.* (Eng.), Sir; Sar Ṭomas Ro = Sir Thomas Roe; Sar Viliyam Noris = Sir William Norris.

Saras, *adj.*, excellent, capital.

Sarasvatī, *f.*, the river Sarasvatī.

Sardār, *m.* (Pers. سَردار), chief, a noble.

Sarīpaṭhe, *adv.*, well.

S'arīr, *n.*, the body.

Sarkār, *f.* (Pers. سَرکار), the Government.

Sarkārī, *adj.* (Pers. سَرکاری), governmental, government.

Sarkh-o, -ī, -uñ, *adj.*, like, similar to.

Sār-o, -ī, uñ, *adj.*, good, well.

Sarovar, *n.*, a lake.

Sāru, *postp.*, for, because of, on account of.

Sarvaśaktimān, *adj.*, Almighty.

Sarve, *adj.*, all.

Sāt, *num. adj.*, seven.

Satā, *f.*, authority (= sattā).

Satārā, *n.*, pr. n. of a town in the Deccan, not far from Poona.

Satāvavuñ, *v. tr.*, to persecute.

Sāthe, *postp.*, with, along with.

Satī, *f.*, the custom of *satī* (suttee), or self-immolation of widows.

Sātm-o, -ī, -uñ, *adj.*, seventh.

Satrāmī, *m.*, pr. n. of a man.

S'atru, *m.*, an enemy.

Sattā, *f.*, authority, influence.

Sattādār, *adj.* (*sattā* — Pers. دار), powerful, influential.

Sau, *adj.*, all; *sau kartāñ*, more than all.

Sāvā, (Ar. ساوة), name of a lake, the water of which is said to have dried up at Muḥammad's birth.

Sāvacheṭ, *adj.*, aware, attentive, expectant.

Savāl, *m.* (Ar. سُوال), question, enquiry.

Savār, *m.* (Pers. سوار), a horseman.

Savār, *f.*, morning.

Savāre, *adv.*, in the morning, early.

S'eher, *n.* (Pers. شهر), a city.

Semenīs, *m.*, pr. name.

Señ, *v. sub.*, so.

Senā, *f.*, an army.

Senāpatī, *m.*, a general.

Sikandar Ādil S'āh, *m.* (Pers. سکندر عادل شاه), pr. n. of a King of Bījāpur.

Sikandar Sur, *m.*, pr. n. of a man.

S'īkhavavuñ / Sikhavavuñ } *v. tr.*, to teach, instruct.

S'īkhvuñ / Sikvuñ } *v. tr.*, to learn.

Sindh, *m.*, pr. n., the province of Sindh.

Sindhunadī, *f.*, the river Indus.

Sipāī, *m.*, a *sipāhī* (sepoy), soldier; *polīs sīpāī*, a native policeman.

S'īr Afgān, (Pers. شیر افغان), Shīr Afghān, pr. n. of a man.

Siriā, *m.*, Syria.

S'ivāe, *postp.* (Pers. سوای), except,

So, *num. adj.*, a hundred; *ekso*, one hundred. (With higher numbers prefixed this word becomes *señ*, as *baseñ*, two hundred).

S'o, śī, śuñ, *interr. and adj. pron.*, what?

S'obhā, *f.*, ornament, beauty.

S'obhāemān, *adj.*, ornamental, ornamented.

Sogand, *m.* (Pers. سوگند), an oath; *s. khāvī*, to swear (*ek vastuno*, *by* a thing).

S'olingar, *n.*, name of a place.

Somnāth, *n.*, name of a city.

Somvār, *m.*, Monday.

Sonāpur(-por), *n.*, name of a part of Bombay.

Sonuñ, *n.*, gold.

S'rāpit, *adj.*, accursed.

Staneśvar, *n.*, name of a town, 50 miles N. of Pānīpaṭ.

Sthāpnā, *f.*, establishment, founding.

Sthāpnār, *m.*, a founder, establisher.

Sthāpvuñ, *v. tr.*, to establish, found.

Strī, *f.*, a woman.

Sūbo, *m.* (Pers. صوبه), a province; a petty ruler.

S'uddh / S'udh } *adj.*, pure, clean.

Sūdhāro, *m.*, a reform, an improvement.

S'uddhatā, *f.*, purity, cleanness.

Sudhī, *postp.*, until, as far as, up to.

S'uddhpaṇuñ, *n.*, purity, cleanness.

Sujā, *m.* (Ar. شجاع) pr. n. of a prince.

S'ukan, *n.*, an omen, portent; *śukan jonār*, a diviner.

Sukāvavuñ, *v. tr.*, to dry up.

Sukāvuñ, *v. intr.*, to dry up, wither; *sukāī javuñ*, to dry up.

Sukh, *n.*, happiness, comfort.

Sukhī, *adj.*, happy, comfortable.

Sultān, *m.* (Ar. سُلْطَان), Sultan.

S'uñ, *pron. interr. n.*, what? (often used as the sign of a question).

Sundar, *adj.*, beautiful, fair.

Sūro, *m.*, a brave man, a hero.

Suvnuñ, *v. intr.*, to sleep.

Svabhāv. *m.*, nature.

Svabhāvik, *adj.*, natural.

Svādhīn, *adj.*, subject, subjected; *s. karvuñ*, to render subject.

Svapaṇuñ, *n.*, a dream.

Svār, *m.* (Pers. سوار), a horseman.

Svarg, *n.*, the sky, heaven.

Svārī, *f.*, an expedition, incursion.

Svatantrapaṇ, *n.* } independence.
Svatantratā, *f.* }

T and Th (ત and થ).

Tābe, *adj.* (Ar. تابع), obedient.

Tadbīr, *f.*, plan, device.

Taiyār, *adj.* (Urdū تيّار), ready, prepared.

Taiyārī, *adj.* (Urdū تيّاري) preparation.

Tājmehel, *n.*, the Tāj Mahal at Agrā.

Taḷe, *postp.*, under, beneath, below.

Talvār, *f.*, the sword.

Tamār-o, -ī, -uñ, *poss. pr.*, your, yours.

Tambu, *m.*, a tent.

Tame, *pron.*, you (*v.* gr.).

Tandarost, *adj.* (Pers. تندرست), healthy, well.

Tane, *pron.*, to thee, thee (*v.* gr.).

Tāñhāñ, *adv.*, then.

Tapās, *f.* (Ar. تَفَحُّص), enquiry, investigation.

Tapāsvuñ, *v. tr.*, to enquire, examine into, inspect.

Taraf, *f.*, direction (Ar. طرف); *postp.*, towards.

Tāre, *adv.*, then (*v. tyāre*).

Tāre, *pron.* (form of *tuñ*, thou), to thee (*v.* gr.).

Tareh, *f.* (corr. from Ar. طَرْح), manner, method.

Tarīk (Ar. طريق), method.

Tār-o, -ī, -uñ, *pron.*, thy, thine.

Tāro, *m.*, a star.

Tart, *adv.*, at once, immediately (also *turt*).

Tārthī (*tāre* + *thī*), from that time.

Tātār, *m.*, Tātār (Tartar).

Tathā, *conj.*, and.

Te, *demonst. m. f. n.*, that; *pron.*, he, she, it; *neut. pl.*, they (*v.* gram., Pronouns); *tethī*, from that, on that account (also *tethī karīne*, id.).

Teḍuñ, *n.*, invitation; *t. karvuñ*, to invite.

Teko, *m.*, a prop, support; *teko āpvo*, to give support, to uphold, prove.

Telicharī, *n.*, name of a place.

Tem, *adv.*, thus; *pron. obl.*, them.

Temaj, *adv.*, thus; *conj.*, just as, as well as.

Teṇī, *she*: teṇi-no, -nī, -nuñ (*v.* gr. *sub. pron. pers.*), her, hers.

Tevaṇ, *pron.* (Pārsī-Guj.), he.

Tev-o, -ī, -uñ (*correl.* to *jevo*, q. v.), as, such as.

Thāṇeśvar, *n.*, pr. n. of town, Thāneśvar.

Thavuñ, *v. intr. aux.* (*v.* gr.), to become.

Thī, *postp.*, from, by, through.

Thoḍ-o, -ī, -uñ, *adj.*, few, a few.

Tīkh-o, -ī, -uñ, *adj.*, hot, quick-tempered; pungent.

Tīkshṇabuddhī, *f.*, keenness of intellect, sharpness, cleverness.

Tiraskār, *m.*, contempt, aversion.

To, *particle*, then (donc), *correl.* to *jo*, if.

Toḍvuñ, *v. tr.*, to break, fracture; *toḍī pāḍvuñ*.

Tohomat, *f.* (Ar. تهمة), accusation, false charge.

Topaṇ, *conj.*, nevertheless, yet.

Traṇ, *num. adj.*, three.

Trīj-o, -ī, uñ, *adj.*, third.

Trimbak Rāy, *m.*, pr. n. of a Marāṭhā.

Trinomālī, *n.*, name of a place.

Tuvār, *m.*, pr. n. of Rajpūt family (Kings of Delhi).

Tuñ, *pron.*, thou.

Turkastān, *n.*, Turkistan.

Turkī, *adj.*, Turkish.

Turt, *adv.*, at once, immediately.

Turtvelā, *adv.* (Pārsī), immediately, at once.

Tyāñ, *adv.*, those.

Tyāre, *adv.*, then (*v. tāre*).

Tyārbād, *adv.* (*tyār* and Ar. بعد), afterwards.

Ṭ and Ṭh (ટ and ઠ).

Ṭakāv, Ṭakāvo, *m.*, stability, durability.

Ṭānṭīo, *m.*, the leg.

Ṭhagāī, *f.*, defrauding, cheating, robbery.

Ṭhāṇo, *m.*, Tanna, a place not far from Bombay.

Ṭharāv, *m.*, decision, resolve.

Ṭharāvavuñ, *v. tr.*, to decide, fix, settle, appoint.

Ṭheravavuñ, *v. tr.*, to fix, resolve, appoint.

Ṭoḍarmal, *m.*, pr. n. Rājā Ṭoḍarmal; a celebrated Hindū of Akbar's time.

U (Ŭ & Ū) (ઉ & ઊ).

Ubh-o, -ī, -uñ, *adj.*, standing upright; *ubho thavo*, to stand up.

Uchār, *m.*, pronunciation.

Udepur, *n.*, pr. n. of city, Udaipur (Oodeypore).

Udyañsing, *m.*, pr. n. of a prince.

Ujās, *m.*, light, splendour, lustre.

Ujjeṇ, *n.*, city of Ujjain.

Ulaṭpālaṭ / Ulaṭpūlaṭ } *adj.*, across; *subs. f.*, revolution; *āropīe sākshīne ulaṭ pālaṭ tapāsvānī nā pāḍī*, the accused refused to cross-examine the witness.

Ulṭ-o, -ī, -uñ, *adj.*, reverse, contrary, opposite.

Umar, *f.* (Ar. عُمْر), age.

Umarāv, *m.* (Ar. اُمَرا, *pl.* of أَمِير), a noble.

Unch-o, -ī, -uñ, *adj.*, high, lofty, noble.

Unḍ-o, -ī, -uñ, *adj.*, deep.

Unṭ, *m.*, a male camel.

Upaj, *f.*, profits, produce, nett gain.

Upadeś, *m.*, teaching, doctrine.

Upar, *postp.*, over, upon.

Upāy, *m.*, resource, remedy.

Upayog, *m.*, use;—*no upayog karvo*, to use.

Upl-o, -ī, -uñ, *adj.*, above, above-mentioned.

Urāvavuñ, *v. tr.*, to cause to fly; to waste, drive away, repel.

Utarvuñ, *v. intr.*, to descend, come down.

Uṭhvuñ, *v. intr.*, to arise, rise, stand up.

Utpann, *adj.* (Sk. *past part.*), created; *utpann karvuñ*, to create.

Uttam, *adj.*, very good, best.

Uttar, *adj.*, northern; *subs. m.*, the north.

Uttar, *m.*, answer; *uttar devo*, to answer.

Uttejan, *n.*, excitement, encouragement; *u. āpvun*, to encourage.

V (વ).

Vachan, *n.*, word, saying.

Vachche, *postp.*, between.

Vadhu, *adj.*, more, greater, further; *vadhu tapās multavī rahī hatī*, the further hearing of the case was postponed.

Vadhāre, *adj.* and *adv.*, more.

Vadhārvuñ, *v. tr.*, to add, increase.

Vadhelo, *m.*, pr. n. of Rajpūt family (kings of Gujarāt).

Vadhvuñ, *v. intr.*, to increase, advance.

Vaḍhvuñ, *v. tr.*, to fight, quarrel.

Vaḍ-o, -i, uñ, *adj.*, great, elderly, eldest.

Vaḍuñ karvuṇ, to extinguish; *vaḍuñ thavuñ*, to go out, depart.

Vagar, *postp.*, without, except; *vagarbhaṇelo*, untaught.

Vagere (corr. from Ar.-Pers. وَغَيْرَه), &c.

Vahāḍyā, *nī galī*, name of a lane in Bombay.

Vāheb, *m.*, pr. n. of an Arab (Wāhib واهب).

Vaihindgaḍh, *n.*, pr. n. town and fort of Vaihindgaṛh.

Vājabī, *adj.* (Ar. واجب), necessary, proper, suitable.

Vajīr, *m.* (Ar. وزير), a Wazīr, minister of state.

Vakht, *m.* (Ar. وقت), time.

Vaḷagvuñ, *v. tr.*, to embrace; to possess (of a devil).

Valāṇ, *f.*, a turn, bend; *v. levī*, to turn (*intr.*).

Vaḷī, *adv.*, again; further, moreover.

Vallabhasen, *m.*, pr. n., Crown Prince of Chāmunḍ.

Vaḷvuñ, *v. intr.*, to be profited, be gained, result.

Vāḷvuñ, *v. tr.*, to bend, fold, dress.

Vañchāvuñ, *v.* (*pass.* of *vāñchvuñ*, q. v.), to be read.

Vāñchvuñ, *v. tr.*, to read.

Vāṇī, *f.*, a voice.

Vañś, *m.*, lineage, family, pedigree.

Vañśāvaḷī, *f.*, genealogy, family line, line of descent, genealogical tree.

Vār, *f.*, period of time.

Varakā, *m.*, pr. n. (Ar. ورقة), Waraqah.

Varas, *n.*, a year (*v. varsh*).

Vāras, *m.* (Ar. وارث) an heir.

Vāraso, *m.*, inheritance, heritage (corr. from Ar. وارث, heir, ورث, heritage).

Vārevār, *adv.*, from time to time, continually.

Varsh, *n.*, a year (*v. varas*); raining.

Vaś, *adj.*, subdued; *v. karvuñ*, to subdue.

Vasnāro, *m.*, a dweller, inhabitant (*f. vasvuñ*).

Vastī, *f.*, abode; population.

Vastu, *f.*, a thing.

Vasvuñ, *v. intr.*, to dwell.

Vasūl, *f.*, revenue; (Ar. وصول), *vasūl karvuñ*, to collect revenue.

Vāt, *f.*, word, matter; story, tale; conversation.

Vay, *f.*, age, period of life.

Vayākaraṇ, *n.*, grammar.

Vazīr, *m.* (Ar. وزير), a Wazīr (Vizier).

Vechvun, *v. tr.*, to sell.

Vehem, *n.* (Ar. وهم), imagination.

Vehemī, *adj.*, imaginative, imaginary.

Vehevuñ, *v. intr.*, to flow.

Veḷā, *f.*, time.

Ver, *n.*, enmity, revenge; *v. levuñ*, to take vengeance.

Verī, *m.*, an enemy.

Vero, *m.*, tax, impost, taxation.

Vepār, *m.*, trading, commerce; *vepārdhandho*, *m.*, commercial business.

Vesh, *m.*, appearance, aspect, garb.

Vichār, *m.*, thought, reflection, consideration.

Vichārvuñ, *v. tr.*, to think, reflect, consider, fancy.

Vidhvā, *f.*, a widow.

Vidyā, *f.*, knowledge, learning.

Vijayrāy, *m.*, pr. n., Vijaypāy, name of a king.

Vikhyāt, *adj.*, renowned, famous.

Vinā, *postp.*, without (*sine*).

Viś, *num. adj.*, twenty.

Viśe } *postp.*, concerning, re-
Vishe } garding.

Vikhervuñ } *v. tr.*, to scatter,
Vinkhervun } disperse.

Viśvās, *m.*, belief, faith; *viśvās lāvo, karvo*, to believe (*—par*).

Y (ય).

Yād, *f.*, memory, recollection; *tene yād āve chhe*, it occurs to his memory; *tene yād rehe chhe*, he remembers (Pers. ياد).

Yāddāst, *f* (Per. يادداشت), memory, power of recollection.

Yādgārī, *f.* (Pers. يادگاری), memorial

Yogya, *adj.*, worthy (of = *ne*).

Yojnā, *f.*, plan, arrangement.

Yojvuñ, *v. tr.*, to plan, arrange, devise.

Yukti, *f.*, plan, trick, device.

Z (ઝ).

Zaid, *m.* (Ar. زيد), Zaid, Muḥammad's adopted son.